PRAISE FOR *PLAYING WITH FIRE*

"Here's a sober, scriptural, and altogether fascinating exploration of demonic forces in which journalist Billy Hallowell answers the questions so many people harbor. It's provocative, insightful, and enlightening—a foray into an often-neglected topic that merits more attention than it typically receives. If you want a solid biblical perspective, this is a helpful resource for you."

—LEE STROBEL, *NEW YORK TIMES* BESTSELLING
    AUTHOR OF *THE CASE FOR CHRIST*

"Curious about ghosts, demons, and other invisible enemies? Investigative journalist Billy Hallowell unearths a graveyard of information about spiritual warfare, scary stories, and biblical perspectives on what animates evil in the world and may change your mind about what makes things go 'bump' in the night!"

—KIRK CAMERON, ACTOR AND DIRECTOR

"*Playing with Fire* tackles an intensely difficult topic but does so in an understandable and relatable way. Journalist Billy Hallowell weaves together some of the most challenging biblical questions—and answers—on the spiritual warfare front, leaving readers with quite a bit to ponder."

—JASON ROMANO, AUTHOR OF *THE UNIFORM OF*
    LEADERSHIP, FORMER PRODUCER AT ESPN, AND
    HOST OF THE *SPORTS SPECTRUM* PODCAST

"Riveting! Through fascinating real-life stories and provocative interviews with pastors and theologians, Billy unpacks the complex faith elements underpinning our essential biblical struggle against evil, and relates them to our culture and daily lives."

—KEVIN AND SAM SORBO, ACTORS AND
    AUTHORS OF *TRUE FAITH*

"Billy Hallowell has crafted a book that intelligently responds to an age-old question: Do demons exist, and if so, what or who are they? His intriguing mix of well-documented case studies of demonic activity, interviews with experts, and solid biblical scholarship removes the Hollywood mystique and caricatures to present a thoughtful, well-documented assessment of the reality of good and evil. If you have yearned for something to help you understand this topic, pick up Billy's book and find some answers."

—JOE BATTAGLIA, BROADCASTER, PRODUCER, AND AUTHOR OF *THE POLITICALLY INCORRECT JESUS* AND *UNFRIENDED*

"Understanding evil is essential, yet much of our culture ignores or misrepresents spiritual struggles. In *Playing with Fire*, Billy Hallowell dives deep into an arena that is often overlooked, offering people compelling evidence, witness accounts, heart-stirring claims, and biblical reflections that hold the power to wake readers, inspire their faith, and guide them on a path toward healing. *Playing with Fire* is a must-read."

—SAMUEL RODRIGUEZ, PASTOR AND AUTHOR OF *YOU ARE NEXT*

"Investigative journalist Billy Hallowell is not your average guy. He doesn't play it safe or stick to lightweight topics. He's a reporter who isn't afraid to dive into nightmares to see what hidden treasures he may find in the shadows. His dreams are of a different sort. Today the American Dream is the 40/40/40: work 40 hours a week for 40 years to retire on 40 percent of your income, get your 401k, get a timeshare in Palm Springs, tool around in a golf cart, then claim your spot in the cemetery. But my friend Billy isn't afraid to lead his life in a different direction. He wants to explore the angelic world, both light and dark. He's the kind of guy who delves into demonology, the theological underpinnings of psychospiritual and transrational warfare, and share his insights with a world waiting to hear his fascinating take on all things ethereal. Get ready for your brain to reel at Billy's penetrating insights in *Playing with Fire*."

—BEN COURSON, TV HOST AND AUTHOR OF *OPTIMISFITS*

"Billy Hallowell is a lightning rod. He is the proverbial metal rod mounted on the structure of our modern society intended to protect it from a strike. Hallowell is standing in the middle of a cultural divide shouting Truth at the top of his lungs. To some this makes Hallowell a trouble-maker, to others he is the lone sane voice in the chaotic echo chamber that is our social media and political landscape. In his latest book, Billy Hallowell does it again, explaining a side of Christianity that Hollywood loves to explore and that most of us choose to ignore, either because it's too scary or too weird. We have the record of at least thirty miracles that Jesus performed, including healing the sick, raising the dead, feeding the masses, altering nature itself, and on several occasions Jesus cast out demons. If the Son of Man takes demonic possession seriously, perhaps we should too."

—KRISTOFFER POLAHA, ACTOR, *JURASSIC WORLD 3, WONDER WOMAN*, 1984

PLAYING
WITH
FIRE

PLAYING
WITH
FIRE

A Modern Investigation into
Demons, Exorcism, and Ghosts

BILLY HALLOWELL

EMANATE
BOOKS

Published in Nashville, Tennessee, by Emanate Books, an imprint of Thomas Nelson. Emanate Books and Thomas Nelson are registered trademarks of HarperCollins Christian Publishing, Inc.

Thomas Nelson titles may be purchased in bulk for educational, business, fund-raising, or sales promotional use. For information, please e-mail SpecialMarkets@ThomasNelson.com.

Unless otherwise noted, Scripture quotations are taken from the Holy Bible, New International Version®, NIV®. Copyright © 1973, 1978, 1984, 2011 by Biblica, Inc.® Used by permission of Zondervan. All rights reserved worldwide. www.Zondervan.com. The "NIV" and "New International Version" are trademarks registered in the United States Patent and Trademark Office by Biblica, Inc.®

Scripture quotations marked ESV are from the ESV® Bible (The Holy Bible, English Standard Version®), copyright © 2001 by Crossway, a publishing ministry of Good News Publishers. Used by permission. All rights reserved.

ISBN 978-0-7852-3451-7 (eBook)
ISBN 978-0-7852-3450-0 (TP)

Library of Congress Control Number: 2020939128

Printed in the United States of America

20 21 22 23 24   LSC   10 9 8 7 6 5 4 3 2 1

CONTENTS

CONTENTS

INTRODUCTION
Pop Culture's Obsession with the Demonic

Spinning heads. Levitating bodies. Otherworldly strength. Unrestrained behavior. Gratuitous violence. Eerie voices spouting off vicious claims and threats. These are just some of the themes surrounding demonic possession that Hollywood simply cannot get enough of.

Year after year, Tinseltown churns out an array of films and TV shows that explore evil and the occult, showing how dark forces can upend the lives of unsuspecting characters.

Hollywood's fascination with this topic is understandable considering the age-old struggle against evil that has persisted throughout the millennia—a phenomenon that humans have almost universally grappled with since the beginning of time.

As psychiatrist Richard Gallagher has noted, "Anthropologists agree that nearly all cultures have believed in spirits, and the vast majority of societies (including our own) have recorded dramatic stories of spirit possession."[1]

That's what makes the many plotlines surrounding possession, infestation, and evil so intriguing to audiences. At a base level, there's a timelessness to these phenomena—a relatability that has permeated both culture and history. And when you mix that reality with some people's penchant for being entertained through thrilling and terrifying story lines, you can see why Hollywood won't stop churning out this content, even as culture continues to secularize and seemingly move away from God.

But while people enjoy becoming terrified through entertainment, there's a question at the core of this allure: Are some of these over-the-top themes based in reality? Movies and TV shows have a tendency to show some outlandish events surrounding the existence of evil, but, as Gallagher and many others have contended, claims that mirror this chaos have been made since the dawn of time.

Gallagher, a well-respected psychiatrist who works with the Catholic Church to help spot cases of demonic possession, reported that different cultures have had "varying interpretations," but that "multiple depictions of the same phenomena in astonishingly consistent ways offer cumulative evidence of their credibility."[2] This is a stunning claim from a respected medical professional. And Gallagher's observations aren't exclusive to him, as there are others in the realm of science and medicine who see an undeniable intersection between faith and spirituality.

These dynamics, and the multitude of personal stories that accompany them, leave each of us with a number of options surrounding how we wish to process associated claims.

We are free to dismiss stories involving spirits and the demonic as mere figments of humanity's—and Hollywood's—imagination. We can essentially ignore their purported presence in the real world, dismissing them as the result of rantings from perceived lunatics. We can also choose apathy, or we can begin to seek answers to the implicit questions surrounding evil.

This latter choice is increasingly difficult in our ever-material world as cultural shifts unfolding on the faith and religion front are having a direct impact on how individuals view the importance and relevance of spiritual issues. There's a deep and profound societal shift taking form in America when it comes to allegiance to faith and God. The Pew Research Center has detailed these stunning changes in an extensive study, revealing that the proportion of Americans identifying as Christians continues to decline significantly.[3]

In fact, the data shows that 65 percent of Americans now call themselves Christians, down from 71 percent in 2014 and 78 percent in 2007. At the same time, the share of people who say they are agnostic, atheist, or "nothing in particular" (a collective group known as the nones) has ballooned from 17 percent in 2009 to 26 percent.

Church attendance is also declining, with 45 percent of Americans saying they attend at least weekly, down from 54 percent in 2009. The changes are multifaceted—particularly when it comes to the nones, but Pew breaks down some of the finer details:

> Both Protestantism and Catholicism are experiencing losses of population share. Currently, 43% of U.S. adults identify with Protestantism, down from 51% in 2009. And one-in-five adults (20%) are Catholic, down from 23% in 2009. Meanwhile, all subsets of the religiously unaffiliated population—a group also known as religious "nones"—have seen their numbers swell. Self-described atheists now account for 4% of U.S. adults, up modestly but significantly from 2% in 2009; agnostics make up 5% of U.S. adults, up from 3% a decade ago; and 17% of Americans now describe their religion as "nothing in particular," up from 12% in 2009.[4]

As people move away from Christianity and church and more toward apathy, materialism, and secularism, there's an implicit assumption that the focus on and exploration of spiritual matters will be increasingly more muted. If one denies God's existence or is simply uninterested in spiritual matters, the expectation is that this person is less interested in believing in or even entertaining the purported roots of evil. To a degree, this is surely true.

Yet despite these changes, audiences still seem enthralled with cinematic explorations of the demonic. Speaking of the horror genre more generally, *Variety* reported that "horror is on a hot streak for the movie business," as terrifying flicks magnetically attract a diverse audience.[5]

Driven potentially by millennials (a group that research has found to be less religiously affiliated than any previous generation), the horror movie industry has been booming, for the first time ever grossing more than $1 billion at the box office in 2017.[6] The lovers of these films tend to be major moviegoers, too, with one report finding that 44 percent of fans who like paranormal horror films go to the movies more than twelve times annually.[7]

Not all horror films are about the demonic, of course, but it's clear there's an increase in the thirst for films about evil, even while our cultural attachment to Christianity is waning. Bible scholar Dr. Michael Heiser believes there's a deeper reason why this dynamic is unfolding—and it all has to do with the inner cravings of the human soul.

"Whether our militant atheist friends, or the village atheist, wants to admit it, most people—even in the West, even in the cultured post-enlightenment technological society West—most people find a materialistic, 'the only thing that's real is what my five senses can detect' worldview, completely unsatisfying," he said.

People, Heiser believes, are looking for something "bigger" than themselves—an explanation that answers the deeper questions about the "rationale for life" and human meaning. The condensed argument? Even when a society abandons or ignores transcendent truths, people are still thirsting for them.

"Theologically, I think we're hardwired to hunger for something transcendent, a reality outside of ourselves. The pop phrase, I guess, is the 'God-shaped void in all of us,'" Heiser said. "But I think we are hardwired for that, and so people are going to try to fill that with something, and they find the dominant Western worldview really lacking."

WHERE AMERICANS STAND ON THE DEMONIC

So, where do people stand when it comes to the existence of the demonic? Believe it or not, there's been some baseline research done in this area, as well as some new, original research we've done for this book.

For now, let's look at what recent polling reveals. An October 2019 survey from YouGov found that 22 percent of Americans believe that demons "definitely exist," with an additional 24 percent stating that these entities "probably exist"—meaning that

Even when a society abandons or ignores transcendent truths, people are still thirsting for them.

nearly half of respondents (45 percent) believe it's likely demonic entities are real and present, at least in some form.[8] The results for ghosts were similar, with 20 percent of respondents taking a definitive stand that they exist and 25 percent believing they "probably" do.

The survey went a bit deeper, though, and also asked about personal experiences with the spiritual realm, finding that 36 percent of respondents "have personally felt the presence of a spirit or ghost," with 13 percent claiming "they have communicated directly with a ghost or spirit of someone who has died."[9]

The final statistic—one that sheds light into beliefs on infestation (spirits remaining in a particular place rather than inside of a person)—is that 43 percent of American respondents believe ghosts can return to haunt places or even other people.[10]

Going a bit deeper, belief in the existence of Satan has been traditionally prevalent among Americans. A 1998 CBS News poll found that 64 percent of Americans believed in the devil at the time, with the majority—59 percent—also believing that the mind or body could be taken over by Satan or a demon.[11] This possession dynamic, they said, simply couldn't be explained by science or medicine.[12]

Fifteen years later, in 2013, YouGov asked some similar questions, finding that the majority of Americans (57 percent) still believed in the devil, with 28 percent responding that they did not believe in Satan.[13] Meanwhile, more than half—51 percent—said they believed that a person could become possessed by a demon or an evil spirit, though 45 percent said they felt it rarely happens (only 15 percent said it happens "frequently" or "very frequently").[14]

So, while it's clear that society has been secularizing, and it's possible fewer people will express belief in these experiences as time forges on, a sizable portion of the American public acknowledges these sentiments, including more than four in ten Americans still expressing the belief that demons exist.[15]

WHERE CHURCH LEADERS STAND ON SPIRITUAL WARFARE

But what about Christian leaders more specifically? In preparing *Playing with Fire*, a survey was commissioned through HarperCollins Consumer Insights to discern what Christians in church leadership positions believe about demons, ghosts, and a litany of related issues.

The results included church staff, elders, deacons, trustees, board members, ministry leaders, coordinators, volunteers, pastors, priests, clergy, small group and Bible study leaders, and Sunday school teachers. It's a wide-sweeping group, but one with individuals who all share a common thread: they serve in some form as church leadership, helping guide and tend to parishioners' needs.

Overall, the findings are quite telling. The vast majority of church leaders take the Bible at face value, with 82 percent of the 1,187 people surveyed believing that demonic forces have the ability to overtake a person's mind or body, and 85 percent stating that demons are active spirits in the modern era that can harm humans.

Considering the prevalence of these stories in the biblical narrative, this isn't entirely surprising. Four percent said they believe demons are active today but cannot harm humans, with just 1 percent stating that they can no longer harm human beings; 9 percent were unsure.

One of the theological claims made by a substantial number of theologians and pastors interviewed for this book is that full possession is incredibly rare, but around three in ten of the church leaders surveyed (28 percent) said they believe they have seen first-hand examples of full demonic possession, with more than half—53 percent—saying they have not.

Meanwhile, a similar proportion—31 percent—said they have a close and trustworthy friend or family member who has claimed to experience demonic possession or oppression. The majority of church leaders, though, answered that they did not have such people in their lives.

And what about the cause of these purported afflictions? Church leaders came to some intriguing conclusions on this front. In light of the importance of scriptural warnings about dabbling in the occult (i.e., psychics and divination), 76 percent said such activities could open a person up to full demonic possession.

And more than six in ten (61 percent) said using tools like the Ouija board could also cause similar afflictions, with 52 percent citing "unrepentant sin" as a potential catalyst for demonic manifestations in one's life. A small percentage of church leaders—4 percent—said they do not believe in full possession (we'll get more specific with these definitions later on).

Beliefs about the "treatment" needed to help remedy possession, though, were quite fascinating. Just 1 percent of respondents said possession could be fully explained by modern medicine, with 80 percent saying it could not and 20 percent remaining unsure.

And there was a fair bit of uncertainty when it came to the need for an exorcism (or deliverance) to help someone afflicted of possession, as nearly four in ten (39 percent) church leaders were unsure if these forms of healing are truly needed, though 47 percent answered that they believe this sort of remedy is warranted.

One of the most pressing questions to emerge on this issue is whether Christians—individuals who have truly accepted the Holy Spirit—can experience full possession. The majority of church leaders surveyed agreed with the most prevalent narrative you will see from experts in this book: Christians cannot be fully possessed. Fifty-nine percent said no, 16 percent said yes, and 25 percent were unsure.

The survey also took some intriguing turns on the nature and actions of Satan and demons. Church leaders overwhelmingly said they believe the devil is present and active in today's world (75 percent), with 25 percent of church leaders taking a bit of a different stance: that the devil is representative of general evil in the world. It seems the vast majority of church leaders—87 percent—agree at least somewhat that Satan and demonic forces have the power to negatively impact the broader culture.

And if this is the case, it's remarkable to note that the majority of these leaders also agree at least somewhat (78 percent) that too many pastors and churches ignore issues surrounding spiritual warfare and demons; just 17 percent of the church leaders surveyed said their house of worship has a deliverance ministry. If this is such a sweeping problem, why are so many perceiving their churches as being inappropriately silent?

There was also a widely held belief (87 percent) that demons are fallen angels, with just 3 percent selecting Nephilim as the primary descriptor of these spirits. Interestingly, just 1 percent said demons are the spirits of deceased human beings.

Playing with Fire will also touch on claims surrounding the existence of ghosts, as there is a debate in Christian circles over whether deceased humans can remain behind to haunt people and places. For their part, church leaders mostly deny the notion that a person could die and come back to haunt, with 78 percent rejecting such a prospect and 6 percent believing people can indeed die and come back or remain as ghosts.

We will explore each of these issues in detail, but for now let's circle back to explore the prevalence of possession and demons throughout human history.

Universal Accounts of Possession

The majority of Christians today clearly believe that demons are present and active in our world, but this belief has to some degree had near-universal appearance in almost every culture since the dawn of time.

Like Gallagher, Dr. Craig S. Keener, a professor of biblical studies at Asbury Theological Seminary, believes these experiences are quite common. He wrote in 2010 that "anthropologists have documented spirit possession or analogous experiences in a majority of cultures, although interpretations of the experiences vary."[16]

Keener's study, titled "Spirit Possession as a Cross-Cultural Experience," focused on anthropological reviews and firsthand accounts of possession, and explored whether biblical claims of possession could reflect "genuine eyewitness material."[17] The main takeaway is that spirit possession crosses cultures and, though it might manifest itself in ways specific to each culture, its existence is widely attested to. Keener wrote:

> Whereas the availability of concrete ancient sources regarding customs (my own usual scholarly focus) sometimes relativizes the value of more abstract anthropological approaches to the NT, beliefs in control by a foreign spirit are so common among unrelated cultures that they appear to reflect a common human experience of some sort rather than a mere custom.[18]

Keener noted that anthropologist Erika Bourguignon once sampled 488 societies and found that the majority—74 percent—held beliefs in possession, though, again, the beliefs in how it manifested varied a bit. In the end he said Bourguignon's research pointed to "some sort of common experience."[19]

Others found similar cross-cultural phenomena in these spiritual encounters, noting the prevalence of changes in voice and behavior. And, as Keener detailed, it was also common to observe an afflicted person's failure to remember what had unfolded once he or she left the purported state of possession.[20]

Keener also cited anthropologist Raymond Firth, who detailed seeing "startling" personality changes and behaviors while in the field. These dynamics included "trembling, sweating, groaning, speaking with strange voices, assumption of a different identity, purporting to be a spirit not a human being, giving commands or foretelling the future in a new authoritative way."[21]

To anyone who has read the New Testament, these claims are likely unsurprising, as some of these characteristics are seen in Scripture among those described in the texts as being demonically possessed. We will later explore what the Bible documents about possession, but the broader point worth reaffirming is that there are thousands of years of claims surrounding the existence of demons and possession—and people continue to express these struggles in the modern era.

Some purported cases of alleged possession have been well documented over time. We have already mentioned the biblical accounts. There are also many others like the 1778 exorcism of George Lukins, an English tailor who reportedly started acting in a strange manner. Lukins was said to have spoken in an unfamiliar voice, made strange sounds, and even sang hymns backward.[22]

Then there's the Ammons case, a modern-day possession claim that stands out for somehow making its way into a mainstream newspaper and stirring the intrigue of the nation at large. The situation, which was covered in the *Indy Star* in 2014, focused on a supposedly possessed mother and her children; it immediately went viral.

And considering the claims embedded within—that government officials saw a nine-year-old boy walk up a wall, that a sheriff heard a demonic voice over his radio, and that doctors saw a child exhibit extra-human strength—it's no surprise why the media took note.[23] When the dust settled, though, the topic once again vanished from the mainstream discussion, with very little exploration of what, if anything, was spiritually unfolding.

Cases like Lukins's and Ammons's have understandably been questioned for their veracity, as facts and details matter. But the dismissive handling of these circumstances by some critics can also have a chilling impact on the future sharing of such experiences.

Quite often people remain silent or resort to quietly whispering about what they've seen, heard, or felt for fear of being labeled "insane," "crazy," or for having a debilitating transfixion with the hyperspiritual.

Even as I wrote this book, some declined interviews and opted for silence rather than openly sharing what they claimed to have faced—and that speaks volumes. And who can blame them? The uncertainty and perceived strangeness of these topics often relegates demons, demonology, and discussions of satanic influence to the quiet corners of the human experience.

But a series of important theological questions emerge, especially for those who claim to have a biblical worldview: Are demons real? If so, what are they? Can demons infest locations or control human beings? How, if at all, can Christians be affected? If it's true these malevolent spiritual beings exist, what can be done to stop them?

And the list goes on.

This book relies on a diverse pool of interviews with Christian experts who will collectively take us through the various views and perspectives related to each of these curiosities. We will also explore personal stories from people who believe they were afflicted by the demonic as we navigate the alleged impact of playing with fire.

It is this concept of "playing with fire"—the title of this book—that we can see directly playing out in Scripture, as the Bible repeatedly warns humans against dabbling in the occult. Yet thousands of years later, psychics, mediums, Ouija boards, and other attempts to crack into the spiritual realm still remain wildly popular.

Some will claim these activities are harmless parlor games, though others openly frame them as something far more sinister, warning that engagement in such antics is akin to lighting a fire and being unable to contain the raging blaze that follows.

Scripture specifically implores people to "resist the devil" (James 4:7), but there are also blatant warnings throughout the text that flagrantly tell us not to "practice divination or seek omens" (Leviticus 19:26), not to "turn to mediums or seek out spiritists" (Leviticus 19:31), and not to consult the dead. These verses warn that humans will be "defiled" by such practices.

And in the New Testament, specifically, we see numerous examples of possession that are stirring, traumatic, and difficult to imagine—examples that many experts believe show us the fiery effects that can come when we decide to dabble with fire and find our souls and lives scorched by the fallout.

And while these examples are essential to fully understanding Christian theology, all too often our cultural focus is on *the impact of evil*. Discussions surrounding demons, Satan, and spiritual warfare tend to focus on the more bombastic and shocking elements, but many people are looking for answers—information to satisfy ever-pressing questions surrounding how evil manifests and how people can overcome it and find healing through Christ. Let's begin our journey by exploring some well-known claims of possession and infestation.

PART ONE

REAL-LIFE STORIES

THE EXORCIST

It's hard to overemphasize the monumental impact *The Exorcist* has had on American culture. The nation was captivated in 1973 when the film burst onto the big screen, terrifying moviegoers with the otherworldly story of a little girl who was "possessed by a mysterious entity," sending her desperate mother on a quest to seek priests' help in freeing the child.[1]

The Exorcist, like the litany of horror films that have followed in its path, preyed on the intrigue and fear that people experience when they consider the happenings purported to unfold when the lines blur between the material and spiritual.

But *The Exorcist* is truly unique for a number of important reasons. First and foremost, the film was understandably credited at the time of its release with helping transform the ways in which people processed demonic possession, with Dr. Arnold T. Blumberg explaining the sweeping cultural impact in concise and intriguing form:

The Exorcist casts a substantial shadow over cinema history, but perhaps most significantly of all, it posits a world in which God is most definitely alive and well . . . if not always there to immediately save the innocent from torment.

Despite taking viewers on a nerve-wracking roller-coaster ride of demonic proportions, the film manages to convey an extremely positive message for those with spiritual conviction. After all, the very idea that the Catholic rite of exorcism could work against an actual demon attempting to gain control of a girl's soul confirms that these things are true; therefore, God too must be real. The result is a film that, while horrific, tells the faithful that they are right.[2]

The success and immediate impact of *The Exorcist* was so jarring that the film caught the notice of outlets like the *New York Times*, with 1970s news reports detailing not only its popularity but also some of the pervasive problems the movie was creating for the Catholic Church. After the film's release, a 1974 *Times* piece warned of "terrified teenagers and priests" who were losing sleep as well as a "wave of inquiries" from people worried that they or their loved ones were possessed.

"I've received dozens of calls from people who are horribly frightened or so confused that they have begun to lose their grip on reality," the Rev. Richard Woods, a then-priest at Loyola University, told the *Times*. "I also know of two kids who came out of the movie thinking that they were possessed, and they have now been hospitalized."[3]

Clearly, the impact was immediately widespread and palpable. Decades later, though, the movie is still wildly popular, continuing to petrify viewers across the globe. People are free to debate and discuss the potential reasons *The Exorcist* has both terrified and resonated for decades, but perhaps the most obvious explanation for the endless intrigue and excess attention stems from the real-life history that inspired its plotline.

As it turns out, *The Exorcist* was inspired by the strange, supposedly real-life events surrounding a young boy named Robbie Mannheim (an alias used to protect his real identity)—happenings that were said to have unfolded in 1949 on the campus of Saint Louis University (SLU) in Saint Louis, Missouri.

It was Robbie's weeks-long exorcism there that became the basis of author William Peter Blatty's 1971 book *The Exorcist*, a literary project that went on to inspire the timeless 1973 film by the same name. Ironically, Blatty, who died in 2017, said, "When I was writing the novel, I thought I was writing a supernatural detective story that was filled with suspense with theological overtones. To this day, I have zero recollection of even a moment when I was writing that I was trying to frighten anyone."[4]

Yet Blatty's writings ignited a multigenerational terror-fest, and when you look deeper at the real-life material he was basing it on, it's easy to understand why.

Digging into the purported details of Robbie's story quickly turns into an amalgam of eerie fascination and strange circumstance. Robbie was a fourteen-year-old boy from Mount Rainier, Maryland, in January of 1949, when he started experiencing some truly concerning issues in his life and home.

From scratching sounds on the walls and floor of his bedroom to his mattress moving and other elements, Robbie's family started becoming concerned over the supposedly inexplicable events that were taking shape. A recap of these happenings published in the *St. Louis Dispatch* in 1988 gives a lense into some of the other terrifying claims and behaviors:

> In these nocturnal episodes (the boy's bizarre behavior occurred mostly at night), he would supposedly become incredibly strong, his body distorting and transforming, heels touching the back of his head, the body forming a loop—all reported by priests who were witnesses.

Curiously, during these convulsions, the doctors attending him could find no change in his pulse rate or blood pressure. The bed would shake violently. Obscene words and images appeared on his skin, in raised red welts, like bas reliefs.[5]

There are some theories surrounding the spiritual catalyst for these supposed issues and manifestations. Robbie's Aunt Tillie is named as a family member from St. Louis who was close to the teenager; she was said to have been interested in the occult.[6] Aunt Tillie reportedly introduced Robbie to the Ouija board before her death, based on some accounts. And, according to a St. Louis University retelling of the story, chaos erupted after he tried to use the board to reach Tillie in the afterlife.[7]

This, of course, will be unbelievable to some, as it sounds like it was lifted from a Hollywood script. But so goes the narrative surrounding Robbie's fascinating story. Still, it's important to note that all these details have been passed down from various sources and not from Robbie's own experience, as the boy—who is now elderly—has never publicly spoken about what purportedly befell him.

Regardless of the true cause of these issues, Robbie's family reportedly sought the help of a doctor, a psychiatrist, and a psychologist; they also reached out to a Lutheran minister named Reverend Luther Miles Schulze to help halt the chaos.[8]

Schulze, who apparently wasn't able to tackle the issue himself, sent them to a priest named Father E. Albert Hughes, who some believe unsuccessfully attempted to perform an exorcism and was injured in the process after the boy reportedly broke off a piece of the spring from his mattress and slashed Hughes's arm (the history is a bit murky here, but it appears Hughes was, at the least, deeply shaken by Robbie's affliction).[9]

Continuing on their desperate quest for spiritual healing, the family decided to take Robbie to St. Louis, and that's when the boy's parents connected with SLU. What followed was "one of the most remarkable experiences of its kind in recent religious history," as the *Washington Post* stated in 1949.[10]

Robbie and his family stayed with a relative who went to SLU, and she connected them with Father Raymond Bishop, one of her former professors at the university. After connecting with other leaders and priests at the school, including Father William Bowdern, the decision was made to perform an exorcism on Robbie—a process that took more than a month.

Some sources emphasize that the decision to perform the exorcism and rely on the "supernatural" for a "cure" wasn't made until Robbie was taken to hospitals, with medical professionals claiming he couldn't be cured through normal means.[11]

Bowdern, who led the exorcism, was joined by Bishop, with Bishop keeping a diary of the entire ordeal.[12] Other priests also took part throughout the month-long attempt to rid Robbie of demonic influence—and the real-life claims surrounding the spectacle are just as shocking as anything one would expect to see in a Hollywood horror film.

The twenty-six-page diary has been of great interest over the years, as it details what priests who were present during the exorcism claimed to have viewed and experienced—and, considering the popularity of *The Exorcist*, the purportedly real-life details are coveted.

"What he describes was pretty gruesome, if that's the word," John Waide, a retired archivist at the SLU library, told the *Springfield News-Leader* in 2017. "I don't know what the right word is. It's pretty detailed and pretty graphic. It hits you right in the face."[13]

Some of the entries do appear quite troubling. Perhaps most strangely, Bishop wrote of apparitions and images that purportedly appeared on Robbie's body, including an image of the devil on his leg and the word *hell* popping up on his chest.[14] One specific entry from

March 18, 1949, speaks of the events that unfolded as exorcism prayers were uttered around Robbie:

> The prayers of the exorcism were continued and R was seized violently so he began to struggle with his pillow and the bed clothing. The arms, legs, and head of R had to be held by three men. The contortions revealed physical strength beyond natural power. R spit at the faces of those who held him and at those who prayed over him. He spit at the relics and at the priests' hands. He writhed under the sprinkling of Holy Water. He fought and screamed in a diabolical, high-pitched voice.[15]

Reverend Walter H. Halloran, one of the priests involved in helping with the exorcism, also publicly addressed these claims years later. He revealed some of the events he witnessed, corroborating the claim that he saw the word *hell* emerge on the boy's skin—something that apparently happened "a number of times."

"It wasn't a case of taking a pin and scratching himself," Halloran said. "It just appeared, and with quite a bit of pain."[16] Halloran also confirmed reports that the boy broke the priest's nose during one of these fits—yet another shocking development that was often purported about the perplexing case. One of the most remarkable elements of the case, though, is that Robbie's story almost didn't come to light.

If not for the *Washington Post*'s report, Robbie's case would have likely remained quiet and forgotten, failing to make waves and unlikely to have been the focus of a novel and feature film. But somehow the *Post* caught wind of the exorcism, publishing an August 20, 1949, front-page story titled, "Priest Frees Mt. Rainier Boy Reported Held in Devil's Grip."[17]

The lede of the article, by journalist Bill Brinkley, proclaimed that a boy had "been freed by a Catholic priest of possession by the devil," citing "Catholic sources" as the basis of this news, and noted that it purportedly took twenty to thirty exorcism attempts to ensure that the expulsion was successful.[18]

The article neither names the boy nor cites his alias, Robbie, but it does recount purported claims from the exorcism, including sources' proclamations that the boy "broke into a violent tantrum of screaming, cursing and voicing of Latin phrases," with Brinkley noting that this was a language the boy had not spent any time studying.

By May 1949, Robbie was reportedly ridded of the issues that afflicted him, with the final lines of the *Post* story reading, "Finally, at the last performance of the ritual, the boy was quiet. Since then, it was reported, all manifestations have ceased."[19]

Blatty himself discovered Robbie's story in the *Washington Post* report; it was a tale that stuck with him, with the author coming to believe it would boost people's faith to hear of the intense affliction—and resolution. The author discussed these elements in a 2000 interview with IGN, explaining that he hadn't only read the story but had also heard details about the exorcism during a New Testament course he took at Georgetown.

"Like so many Catholics, I've had so many little battles of wavering faith over the course of my life. And I was going through one at that time," Blatty said. "And when I heard about this case and read the details, that seemed so compelling. I thought, 'My God, if someone were to investigate this and authenticate it, what a tremendous boost to faith it would be.' I thought, 'Someday I would like to see that happen. You know, I would like to do it.'"[20]

As for the infamous diary of the exorcism affair, Blatty told IGN that he had asked for a copy, but that the Cardinal in St. Louis declined him, as the Catholic Church had promised to keep Robbie's identity a secret and wanted no publicity around his story. It wasn't until after *The Exorcist* novel was written that Blatty received a copy from one of the monks involved in the exorcism.[21] But the church's official reluctance to discuss the case further led Blatty to believe it was all a legitimate story.

And he notably claimed Bowdern—the lead exorcist—once wrote him and confirmed that this was truly the case (a remarkable fact, considering that Bowdern reportedly never made any sort of public admission that he was the exorcist involved).[22] "He said, 'I can tell you one thing . . . the case I was involved with was the real thing. I had no doubt about it then. I have no doubt about it now. Good luck with your apolistic pursuits,'" Blatty recounted.[23]

The 1949 *Washington Post* story was apparently a source of contention for Bowdern and others involved in the case, as they felt the situation should have remained a secret. In fact, Reverend William Van Roo, who took part in the exorcism, told the *St. Louis Post-Dispatch* in 1988 that he wishes it would have all stayed under wraps.[24]

"It should have been kept a secret. The whole chronicle was leaked to the *Washington Post*," he said. "The young man has had to suffer so much; it caused severe pain and resentment, because the confidentiality was violated."

To this day, Robbie's real-life identity is not widely known, with the Catholic Church honoring its pledge to seal the relevant files. That said, multiple sources have reported that he went on to lead a normal life; Robbie reportedly got married and had children. There are no sources reporting his death, with most noting he is still living, keeping his identity a secret despite the cultural fascination that stemmed from his ordeal. As we will see, Robbie's story isn't the only one to make an international splash.

THE INDIANA CASE

He walked up the wall, flipped over . . . and stood there." And if that's not strange enough, another eyewitness description proclaimed that a little boy from Indiana "glided backward on the floor, wall and ceiling."[1]

I remember reading those words in a strange state of shock and wonder. How in the world did a little boy allegedly walk up a wall? I wondered. And why was a mainstream outlet like the *Indianapolis Star* covering such a bizarre story?

I had a slew of immediate questions about the 2014 story that had come out of Gary, Indiana, about a so-called demon house that was filled with terrifying tales, but the claim about a little boy walking up a wall was the hands-down, most offbeat detail amid the plethora of strange phenomena surrounding Latoya Ammons and her family.[2]

Much like Robbie's ordeal, the Ammons story was made public through a prominent media outlet. The difference in this case, though, was that some of those impacted willingly spoke out and shared the purported details.

Former *Indy Star* journalist Marisa Kwiatkowski opened her now famous 2014 article on the Ammons case titled "The Exorcisms of Latoya Ammons" by reporting that Ammons and her three children "claimed to be possessed by demons."

The lede was anything but buried, as there were many elements that boldly distinguished the story from other paranormal claims. Among the intriguing facets was the series of prominent people—including a family case manager, a nurse, and veteran police captains—who all seemed to corroborate various pieces of the bizarre puzzle.

So, what exactly unfolded in Ammons's Gary, Indiana, home? According to her own media account, Ammons said she and her family began experiencing strange phenomena just one month after moving into the rental home.

It was December 2011 when large black flies reportedly started swarming the family's porch, coming back again and again even after they were killed. Ammons and her mother, Rosa Campbell, told the *Indy Star* that they also started hearing footsteps coming up from the basement every night—and that it sounded as though the door was repeatedly creaking open.[3]

By March 2012—just four months after moving into the home—the strangeness kicked up a notch. Campbell told Kwiatkowski about a night when the family found one of Ammons's children unconscious and *levitating*. Overwhelmed by the events unfolding in the home, the family sought the help of clairvoyants and local churches. They purportedly burned sage, drew crosses on the hands and feet of the children using olive oil, and attempted various acts recommended to them in an effort to rid the home of the supernatural forces they believed were infesting it.

None of this worked, though, with the family claiming that their problems only worsened. Ammons and her three kids (at the time aged seven, nine, and twelve) all reported experiencing what they described as "possession," with the purported effects reading like a horror novel.

Ammons and Campbell reportedly told Kwiatkowski that "the kids' eyes bulged, evil smiles crossed their faces, and their voices deepened every time it happened."[4] Additionally, the seven-year-old reportedly spoke to another child whom no one else could see.

Ammons soon turned to her children's doctor for help. Her kids' bizarre behavior while in the doctor's office teamed with the family's claims of paranormal activity led medical professionals to call emergency services. "Twenty years, and I've never heard anything like that in my life," Dr. Geoffrey Onyeukwu, the physician involved in the incident, told the *Star*. "I was scared myself when I walked into the room."[5]

An official report details what some medical professionals claimed to have witnessed. The document reads, in part: "Medical staff reported that while the children were at their primary doctor's office the medical staff reported they observed [one of the children] be lifted and thrown into the wall with nobody touching him."

Still, not everyone was convinced something supernatural was at play. In the midst of that chaos, a skeptical individual reportedly called the Department of Child Services to file a complaint, which sparked an investigation into Ammons's mental state (an evaluation by a hospital psychological found "there were no concerns about her mental stability at this time").[6]

That's when DCS case manager Valerie Washington entered the picture—and reportedly saw much of the bizarre behavior for herself. Washington's own account of her interaction with the family included seeing the seven-year-old boy's eyes roll back in his head and watching him growl. At one point, the boy reportedly said the following to his brother, "speaking in a different deep voice": "It's time to die. I will kill you."[7]

This brings us to that pivotal point in the story: the claim that the boy walked up a wall. Washington's official DCS report—an account reportedly backed by Willie Lee Walker, a registered nurse who was in the room, says the following about the encounter with the family: "Child became aggressive and walked up the wall as if he was walking on the floor and did a flip over the grandmother. The episode was witnessed by the psych counselor and DCS worker FCM Washington."[8]

This is a strange line to include in government documentation, but it's an account Walker later confirmed to Kwiatkowski, telling the reporter that the boy "walked up the wall, flipped over and stood there." The nurse added, "There's no way he could've done that."[9]

At another point in the document, the DCS report offers additional details about the purported wall incident:

> [REDACTED NAME] had a weird grin on his face and began to walk backwards while the grandmother was holding his hand and he walked up the wall backwards while holding the grandmother's hand and he never let go. He flipped over and landed on his feet in front of the grandmother and sat down in the chair. A few minutes later he looked up as if he was back to himself.

The report states that Washington and at least one other professional left the room immediately to report what unfolded to a doctor, who "did not believe it."[10] The physician went in the room and asked the boy to walk up the wall, but the child said this was not something he could do and was unable to replicate the act.

At another point, the report recaps strange observations that were witnessed as the children heard their mother describe the efforts she had gone through to remove the purported demonic spirits from her children.[11] From growling and rage on the part of one of the children—and the need for multiple people to get involved to try and stop the boy—the alleged details are, at the least, disturbing:

Ms. Ammons was discussing the event that led her family to the hospital this evening and her 7yr old son [REDACTED NAME] started making noises such as growling when she would speak about the different church's [sic] she visited and call looking for help with the demonic spirits in her children and home. [REDACTED NAME] was on the other side of the curtain in another room and she could hear his sounds. The more Ms. Ammons discussed the churches and the advice she was given on how to kill the spirits her son, [REDACTED NAME] got louder and louder growling until a loud shuffle started in the room next door and the [REDACTED NAME] shouted for her mother to come help.

FCM and Ms. Ammons went to the other room to find [REDACTED NAME] had [REDACTED NAME] (9yrs) in a head-lock choking him. [REDACTED NAME's] eyes were rolling in his head and he was growling and his teeth were showing while he held right to his brother's throat. It took several staff to pry the hands open of [REDACTED NAME] to release [REDACTED NAME].

This chaos led child services to temporarily take the children out of the home until they could assess what was unfolding (the children were returned six months later).[12]

Throughout the process, Ammons maintained her story that something supernatural was unfolding, and she wasn't alone in making such claims. Washington later indicated that the situation profoundly impacted her. "It's taken me a while to move past that," she said of her claim of seeing the boy walk up the wall. "I believe that it was something going on there that was out of the realm of a normal living person."[13]

Others who were initially skeptical also came to the conclusion that they were embroiled in the midst of something truly inexplicable. Former Gary police captain Charles Austin told the *Star* that he was initially skeptical of Ammons's story.[14] After all, Austin, who had at the time been a cop for nearly four decades, had likely seen his fair share of strange scenarios, con artists, and liars. But after spending time at the Ammons home and interviewing people involved, he said he was a "believer."

Austin had a variety of his own claims about the home, including seeing "strange silhouettes" in photos taken on his iPhone and observing the driver's seat in his car move backward and forward on its own, among other odd and seemingly inexplicable occurrences.[15] But it's his claim about what happened one day after he left the Ammons's home that is perhaps most disturbing. Austin told the *Daily Mail* that he was at a gas station when the radio in his police car purportedly started operating on its own.[16]

"I had my police radio, my squad car dash AM/FM radio, my police cell and my iPhone," he said.[17] "I was looking at the pictures I had taken on my iPhone when I made this call and all of a sudden this growling voice came from my AM/FM radio. It said, 'YOU OUTTA HERE,' then a lot of garbled other stuff and static."

Brian Miller, who was the police chief of the nearby Hammond Police Department at the time of these strange occurrences, was in the home numerous times and was present during Ammons's exorcisms—and he, too, described events that are not easily explainable. Miller said he and his partner first visited the house when the family had already moved out due to the strange events. The cops were initially skeptical when Ammons and Campbell met Miller and his partner at the home to investigate the claims being made.

"At first . . . we didn't really believe," Miller said, noting that Ammons generally refused to go inside the home during the investigation; her mother, Campbell, went inside during the first visit and took the cops on a tour to explain all that had purportedly unfolded. "We interviewed her and we both walked out of there," he said. "As we're going back to our cars talking, we said, 'It's a great story, but it's not true. There's nothing true about it.' So, we left."

But then Miller encountered Father Michael Maginot, the priest who handled the subsequent exorcisms. Assuming Maginot would never be able to substantiate any of the fantastical claims, Miller figured he would call the priest, corroborate his skepticism, and finally put the case to rest.

"I thought, 'Well to finish the investigation, I should talk to him because he's not going to be able to corroborate any of this. Then I'm just going to say, well this is all imagination,'" Miller recalled. "So I called him and he said . . . he really felt that there was something in the house."

After Maginot started to recount strange phenomena he had observed, Miller began to think twice and started putting the bizarre pieces together. At that point, he had Campbell's claims, the priest's proclamations, and Washington's stunning report about the boy walking up the wall. But Miller said the proverbial icing on the cake came when he and his partner went back to their offices to listen to audio recordings of their interview with Campbell and Washington that was captured inside the home.

"At one point I was upstairs. I was talking to Valerie Washington and [Campbell]. I was interviewing Valerie and [my partner] was downstairs. Captain Austin from the Gary Police Department came by and the two of them were down in the basement," he said. "They're walking and they're talking, and all of a sudden you hear a voice on his tape recorder just plain as day that says, 'Hey!' and it's very clear."

It was a moment that left the officers "freaked out," considering that the "Hey" was uttered in between the others' voices and was disjointed from the conversations unfolding on the recording. After that, Maginot told the officers he wanted to go back to bless the home, and so the group agreed to return once more—and that's when Miller saw something else.

"I happened to walk upstairs and I walked in the center bedroom and the blinds were bleeding oil," Miller said. "They weren't bleeding from the top of the blinds. They're bleeding from the middle of the blinds." He was shocked by what he saw, and wondered whether someone had intentionally sprayed oil. So he wiped the blinds down and secretly put a Q-tip in the door before closing it.

Miller theorized that the Q-tip would fall if someone went back in to intentionally place more oil on the blinds. Then he kept a close eye on the door as the priest continued his blessing. "When we were done, I walked in and the blinds were bleeding oil again down the middle," he said, noting that the officers investigated around the window both inside and out and were unable to locate a discernible source for the mysterious substance.

"We were freaked out at that point," Miller admitted.

For his part, Maginot has been less than silent about what unfolded during these efforts, giving interviews with various media outlets that corroborated these details. Just consider that Maginot answered affirmatively on live TV when former *Fox News* host Bill O'Reilly asked if he believed the Ammons family had experienced "something unworldly" inside the home—a noteworthy moment to say the least.[18]

And in an interview for this book, Maginot again affirmed many of these details, explaining the issues he experienced in the home and describing in detail the exorcisms that he held in an effort to help rid Ammons of the demons he believed were afflicting her.

When he was first called to the Ammons home, Maginot said Ammons and her mother shared the details of what was purportedly unfolding, and that he, like Miller, personally observed various events inside the home. "The light in the bathroom began flickering on and off and making [an] electronic noise," he said, noting that the actions halted the moment he walked over to take a closer look.

Stranger, though, was his claim that the rods on the Venetian blinds would swing back and forth. Witnessing no wind or discernible reason for the movements, he was perplexed—and even more so when he noticed that the same thing was happening in every room of the home. "They seemed to be almost going in unison, like coordinated swings," he said. "I was kind of amazed that they were swinging together."

As time went on and the investigation persisted, Maginot said he was present with police officers—including Miller—and child protective workers both inside the home and at his church, where some of the exorcisms unfolded.

During one incident detailed in Kwiatkowski's story, a family case manager associated with the situation was inside the home when she touched a strange, oily substance.[19] The article offers an intriguing explanation of what happened next:

> [She] touched some strange liquid she saw dripping in the basement, and said it felt slippery yet sticky between her fingers. [. . .]
>
> [She] said she was later standing in the living room with the rest of the group when her left pinky finger started to tingle and whiten. She complained it felt broken.
>
> Less than 10 minutes later, [she] said she felt as if she was having a panic attack. She couldn't breathe, so she walked outside to wait for the group.

Unprompted, Maginot shared this same story with me, explaining that the case worker "put her pinky on the oil that was dripping and all of a sudden her finger turned white." He said she felt pain and was "very much disturbed" by the incident. And Miller, too, recalled the incident, noting that her finger was suddenly "extremely cold like she'd just put her finger in ice water." He affirmed that "she was freaked out."

Maginot, who never performed any spiritual rituals on the children, said he performed numerous exorcisms on Ammons. "It seemed like it was mainly with her," he said of the oppressive issues, noting that it would seemingly jump to the children. "It was never in two people at the same time."

Maginot alleged that his first effort—a minor exorcism (a prayer meant to break evil influences[20])—resulted in Ammons convulsing every time he placed a crucifix on her; she would purportedly stop convulsing when he removed it. At some moments he said Ammons would also convulse if she was given a cross or something religiously themed to wear. Maginot said she even fell asleep during the final exorcism and awoke to find that whatever was afflicting her was finally gone.

Miller, who was present for some of these rites, mirrored Maginot's descriptions of what unfolded but noted that he's often not sure what to say when people ask what he thought of these religious rites; after all, he didn't have a baseline from which to compare. "I'd seen *The Exorcist* where their heads spin around. . . . It wasn't anything like that," he said. "But she kind of just spiculated, and she was making some guttural sounds."

Maginot assumes that these efforts were successful, as he apparently never heard from Ammons again and believes she was healed. Miller said she later told him that the family was doing well. These details are all clearly shocking to read and cause one to wonder what was truly unfolding inside the home.

And while all these details are certainly curious, one of the most interesting elements of the story was the national and international attention it garnered. The *Indianapolis Star*'s story immediately sparked interest across the globe. The outlandish yet well-sourced claims had journalists begging for interviews and piqued the interest of the public at large.

Ammons herself was shocked by the response, telling the *Star* in a later interview: "I figured . . . that I would get uproar from . . . my hometown, but I never imagined that it would go viral."[21] She also noted that there had been a lot of backlash and that she was "fed up" with it.

Much like Robbie's story, this purported ordeal almost never came to light, as Miller and his partner remained silent for two years after the exorcisms, refusing to openly share their experience. But when his good friend Kwiatkowski caught wind of what happened, the journalist wanted to tell the entire story for the *Indy Star*. At first, Miller refused. He eventually relented, though, on the condition that Kwiatkowski wouldn't share the officers' names, and the shocking story finally came to fruition.

While Miller, Maginot, and others still have no natural explanation for what they saw and experienced, not everyone is so certain. Some psychologists who examined Ammons's kids believed that the children were being influenced by the adults around them.

Stacy Wright, a clinical psychologist who spoke with Ammons's youngest son, wrote in her evaluation that this was "an unfortunate and sad case of a child who has been induced into a delusional system perpetuated by his mother and potentially reinforced" by other adults.[22]

Joel Schwartz, another psychologist who spent time speaking with Ammons's other two children, questioned whether Ammons's daughter was "unduly influenced by her mother's concerns" over paranormal issues inside the home.[23]

But Maginot has a message for critics: the events are well documented and were real. "This is actually documented by people who are professionals who had nothing to do with each other . . . the witnesses to the walking up the wall backwards, the witnesses in the doctor's office," he said. "And then the police officers who got involved in this who also witnessed unexplainable things happening to them."

Critics' claims aside, there was something about Ammons's story and the information surrounding it that led to a unique and authentic public curiosity. That curiosity was so intense that the home was purchased in 2014 by TV host Zak Bagans, who made a documentary about the house and later demolished the structure in 2016, recording the entire spectacle for his film.[24]

Despite the fact that some psychologists and skeptics have reportedly felt the story was inauthentic and had more rational roots, the compelling details and unwavering witness testimony had enough legs for mainstream media and the public at large to at least entertain what was claimed, and that's notable.[25]

3

CRANMER'S CLAIMS

A dark column that glided through the house. Mysterious shadows. A rancid stench. Clocks stopping. A mysterious blood-like substance coating the walls. Broken crucifixes. . . . Children exhibiting signs of possible possession."

I pointedly recall writing these words after an oddly disturbing interview I conducted back in 2014 with Bob Cranmer, a businessman and former commissioner in Allegheny County, Pennsylvania.[1] It wasn't necessarily Cranmer himself who left me a bit startled; it was the details of the story he purported—claims that were intensely eerie and seemingly otherworldly.[2]

As the faith and culture editor of *TheBlaze* at the time, I routinely received tips about a litany of stories, and some centered on claims of demonic possession or infestation. This wasn't a topic I obsessively covered, but it was one that would emerge from time to time, specifically surrounding films like *The Conjuring*, which was released in 2013 and sparked a plethora of attention with its claim to have been based on a true story.

Just months after I covered that film and the deep theological debates surrounding its supposedly real-life inspiration, my boss tipped me off to Cranmer's story and said it might be worth reaching out to him. So I did, and what he told me was spine-chilling to say the least, leaving me with a treasure trove of questions that far outpaced any of the answers Cranmer could provide.

At the time, these subjects surrounding demonic possessions and infestations were still relatively foreign to me, and I found myself spending the bulk of my time trying to understand the underlying issues and potential material explanations.

It is important to note that I have always entered into interviews surrounding these topics with a great deal of skepticism. After all, it is well within the confines of the human heart to manipulate or conjure up ghostly stories in an effort to cash in; the more traumatic and terrifying the supposed experience, the higher the potential financial reward.

Some people who have claimed to be bombarded by the demonic have turned their allegations of hauntings and possessions into lucrative book deals, movies, and other endeavors that hold the power to bring in boatloads of money, all while transfixing and perplexing the public. And to be fair, moneymaking in itself is not necessarily a problem, but if the quest for cash causes embellishments, inaccuracies, or totally manufactured stories, then there's a credibility conundrum. Regardless of motivation, though once someone turns his or her story into a book or movie, some critics are sure to be immediately skeptical of that person's claims.

For these reasons, among others, I have always covered these stories with extreme caution, treating them as what they are: people's personal claims and experiences. The role of a journalist is to uncover and convey stories, not to imbue them with one's own views or to lead readers to accept or deny these accounts.

It's about shedding light on stories about compelling people who claim to have been faced with something unexpected and uncommon, and, in the process, working to vet their stories with as much due diligence as possible. And that's where stories like Cranmer's get quite interesting. Along the way, I spoke with others who were familiar with his purported demonic ordeal, and what I learned was fascinating.

After a number of conversations, I did not encounter anyone who disputed Cranmer's claims; the people I spoke with at the time corroborated everything he said about the purported infestation—another element of the story that left me a bit shocked. So, what exactly did Cranmer claim to endure? The former Pennsylvania politician believes that he and his family were victims of something some Christians call "infestation."

The baseline definition of *infest* gives us some insight into its nature. According to *Merriam-Webster*, it means "to spread or swarm in or over in a troublesome manner," with a secondary definition being "to live in or on as a parasite."[3] Thus, someone could use this definition of infestation to describe a situation in which it is believed that a person—or a place—is being attacked or filled with demonic forces.

And that's exactly how Cranmer would frame it, telling me that familial chaos broke out after he, his wife, and children moved into his lifelong dream home. The *Pittsburgh Post-Gazette* described the purported ordeal as follows:

> They said they've seen blood running down the walls and heard pounding on the walls and mysterious footsteps in the hallways. Family members have awakened with mysterious scratches on their legs or said they've been tripped or pushed by the demon.[4]

The experience reportedly turned so horrific and toxic that the family fled to faith leaders and began holding routine deliverance services inside the home.

The most curious element of Cranmer's case—aside from the otherworldly claims of demonic activity—has been his decision to speak out publicly, especially considering his stature as a well-known politician and business leader in the community.

The perceived risk of openly addressing his experience was not lost on me at the time and remains an interesting element of his story. "The whole thing is bizarre. It's crazy. But I'm telling you skeptics, cynics, whoever you are, this happened and I'm telling you it's all true," Cranmer told me in an interview for this book. "Want to believe it? You don't want to believe it? That's up to you. But it's true."

Cranmer dove deep into the roots of his terrifying ordeal, which he said started decades ago when he learned that the home on Brownsville Road in Pittsburgh was for sale. Cranmer, who grew up in the area, had always admired the house. So when it finally went on the market, his mother, a retired real-estate broker, reached out and let him know—and he was elated and dove right in.

But Cranmer said something strange immediately happened when he and his wife went to view the house. "My wife and I had two of our children with us. At the time, my daughter was four years old and my oldest son was three, and we were in the basement and our three-year-old disappeared," he said. "So, my wife noticed he wasn't with us."

Cranmer said his wife went upstairs and found the little boy standing halfway up a staircase. "He was trembling," he recalled. And that's when one of the owners asked a strange question: "Oh, honey, what's wrong? Did you see something?" Cranmer and his wife found the interaction deeply strange. *"See something?"* What would the boy have seen?

Despite the odd moment, the couple went on to buy the house in 1988. After the purchase, Cranmer recalled asking the owner if there was anything wrong with the home. "His answer was odd, because he didn't make me clarify what defined 'wrong,'" Cranmer said. "He right away said, 'Oh, no, we've had mass in the living room twice; house is fine.'"

Cranmer assumed that celebrating Catholic mass inside one's home was a relatively uncommon practice, but he shrugged it off at the time, and the family proceeded to move into their dream home. Unfortunately, he said it took mere weeks before strange occurrences started to unfold. The first event, which was relatively benign, involved a pull-chain and light bulb in a walk-in closet underneath a staircase in the home.

"I noticed when I would reach in to turn that light on . . . I would reach for that chain and I could never find it, because it would be wrapped around the light," he said, noting that at first he assumed his wife was pulling the chain and letting it recoil. But his wife said she hadn't been in the closet, so he left the chain down and did a bit of a test, returning home later in the day to again find it wrapped around the light. The problem persisted until Cranmer tied a wire to the chain and attached it to a coat hook.

"So that began a whole number of seemingly innocuous-type things that would happen on a regular basis that didn't seem threatening," he said. "But nonetheless, we knew there was a spirit in the house."

Not long after purchasing the home, Cranmer said he and his wife brought a priest into the house for a blessing, and something strange happened when the faith leader approached his three-year-old boy's room.

"He wouldn't let the priest in. So we didn't make an issue. The priest just threw holy water on the door and we went by," he said. "Years later, I had come to find out that [a] doctor would use [that room] to perform abortions . . . a lot of death was in that room; it was bad and the previous owners hadn't ever used it as a bedroom."

As time went on, Cranmer said that whatever was in the house started to deeply impact the family, with nervous breakdowns and dysfunction abounding. The initial blessing of the home did nothing to stem the tide of chaos that came in subsequent years.

Around the year 2000, the situation hit a fever pitch. "Things are flying through the air," he said. "The whole family was just in total disarray and this thing unmasked itself for what it was—furniture moving around, it was crazy."

Cranmer said he's not sure what changed inside the home, but that the intensity of the situation left him searching for a remedy. Unfortunately, his Baptist pastor at the time reportedly wanted nothing to do with the situation.

"I said, 'I'm really dealing with some bad evil stuff here. It's bad. I need help,'" Cranmer recounted, but he said the preacher didn't seem to buy his claims. So Cranmer turned to his friend who was the mayor of Pittsburgh at the time to get help connecting with the Diocese of Pittsburgh, a move that officially started the long effort to cleanse the home.

"It got nuts then," Cranmer said. "Absolutely nuts."

He believes demonic forces in the home impacted the mental health of his family, with two of his kids going in and out of psychiatric hospitals. Meanwhile, the physical happenings were terrifying the family. "[There was] insane stuff every day—furniture being moved around, pictures being turned sideways on the walls," Cranmer said. "I'd wake up in the morning and the change on my dresser would all be standing on end, lined up, things that just, you knew you were, like, living with the invisible man."

He said the family would play Mel Gibson's *The Passion of the Christ* on DVD in one of the rooms in an effort to try and expel the spiritual forces, and would come home to find the DVD off and taken out of the player. And it doesn't end there. Cranmer added that the entity would make itself known with a terrible stench; one of his kids even reported seeing the figure in bodily form, describing it as looking "like a woman with long, black hair and a black dress like a nun." There was also a mysterious red substance that would appear in puddles on the floor of the home and on the walls, mirroring the throwing of holy water.

Perhaps the strangest part of the story, though, surrounds an area underneath steps in the home—a location Cranmer described as being completely closed off with drywall, with "not even a crack" of space into the opening. He said the space had been walled off in 1909. This area, in the middle of the home, was believed to be a center of focus for the demonic entity, so a crew came in during this chaotic time and cut a hole into the drywall; they found a number of items inside the previously closed-off area.

"I did find some . . . of my son's Legos in there," Cranmer said. "We found some weird playing cards. We found the skeleton of a bird. We found this piece of amber." How these items found their way through a closed-off wall left Cranmer and his family absolutely stumped. These intensified issues persisted for more than two years from the end of 2003 through 2006, with priests coming into the home every seven to ten days, spending hours inside in an effort to halt the chaos. But after the first year of attempts to cleanse the home, the situation worsened.

Cranmer said his approach began to change and that he and his family started to mock the entity, telling it that it needed to leave "in the name of Jesus" and that the family wasn't planning to back down. Over time, he said its power seemed to diminish. It was not until 2006, though, that the Catholic Church reportedly brought in an exorcist and the final confrontation and expulsion unfolded, with the family holding a mass in the basement of the home, where the entity seemed to be confined.

From there, Cranmer said the issues improved, though there were some random events that popped up here or there in the following years. Each time, he struggled and stressed, fearing the demonic entity would return. "The exorcist pointed out that they do hang around for a while. They tried to come back in," Cranmer said. "So, a few things would happen for a number of years, but it became less and less and less."

Cranmer, who still lives in the home, believes it has been healed.

No matter where people stand on this wild story, there is an important question worth pondering. If these details are true and a demonic force was inside the home, how did that force come to be there? What granted that demon legal rights to do what was being done inside the home? Cranmer has some theories.

As he explored the history of the home, he said he encountered a plethora of strange details about past events and inhabitants—sinister stories that he believes could have been a catalyst for all that he and his family experienced. While researching, Cranmer said he stumbled upon information about the aforementioned abortion doctor who reportedly performed procedures inside the home. Additionally, he learned about another story involving the murder of a mother and her three daughters on the property back in the late 1700s.

Cranmer started digging through the National Archives and discovered that there were major disputes and uprisings between newfound Americans and Native Americans in the post–Revolutionary War era; he also found a letter from U.S. commander Isaac Craig to Secretary of War Henry Knox dated March 31, 1792.[5]

"[The commander] was writing about what was going on and that the Indians were across the river and that he needed more troops and more men," Cranmer said. "In the last couple of sentences to add emphasis to how bad things were, he said this past week, some miles from the Fort, a mother and her three . . . children were slain by the Indians."

As the story goes, the woman and her three children were buried on the property where his home currently stands. So Cranmer set off to try and find physical evidence, hiring Ground Penetrating Radar Systems Inc., a ground penetrating radar company, and the results left him stunned. "Sure enough, six feet down, they showed me there are the outlines of four, one large and three smaller bodies in the ground," he said, noting that he believes this to be the grave.[6]

Cranmer now contends the purported murders, along with illegal abortions that are said to have taken place inside the home in the 1920s and 1930s, invited evil to the land.

Without a doubt, Cranmer's claims will seem strange and unbelievable to some, which again causes one to wonder why he chose to come forward in the first place, especially in light of his stature as a well-known Pennsylvania politician. He admits that he was hesitant at first but felt it was important to share his experience. "I just took a deep breath and said, 'God, if this is what you want me to do, I'm going to do it,'" Cranmer said.

The cost of speaking up about a purported issue like this is certainly steep, despite the monetary value one can yield when it comes to books and movies. In addition to general reputational harm, there is the risk of being publicly maligned, having your sanity questioned—or, at the least, having your story disputed.

It should be noted that some former residents of Cranmer's home have gone on the record to say that they did not experience any supernatural issues inside the home during their tenures. Two families who lived there prior to Cranmer and his family told the *Pittsburgh Post-Gazette* that Cranmer's claims about what unfolded in the home—paranormal experiences previous families had purportedly faced—were based on supposed discussions with their now-deceased parents.[7]

Karen Dwyer lived in the home for seven years in the 1950s and 1960s after her mother divorced and moved in with her parents, but Dwyer said her family never mentioned anything about paranormal activities inside the home; other family members agreed. "My mother never said anything about the house being haunted. My grandmother never said anything about the house being haunted,"

Dwyer told the *Gazette*. "And my grandfather never said anything about the house being haunted."[8]

Another man named Michael Joyce, who lived in the home from age five until age fourteen when his parents sold it to the Cranmers, said that he also has "no evidence of anything like [Mr. Cranmer's claims] ever happening in the house."[9] Of course, this sparks a he said–she said that does little to speak to the legitimacy of Cranmer's own experiences in the home. Regardless of the debate surrounding claims like Cranmer's purported infestation, some experts like Pastor Chad Norris do report encountering these issues where locations—not just people—are deeply impacted by the demonic realm.

"What happens is, people cooperate with the demonic on the Earth [and] that draws them into specific locations," Norris said. When asked if cases similar to Cranmer's, where people have committed a concentration of evil activity, can cause demons to remain in place, Norris answered affirmatively.

Others like the Reverend Benjamin McEntire also spoke about the prevalence of infestation, something that he said is "extraordinarily common" and more prevalent than full possession. "I've spoken to several exorcists who had very long careers . . . who all said that they dealt with the infestation of places, as a pretty much routine matter," he said, "but then would only see a handful of cases that would meet the standard of possession over the course of their career as an exorcist."

One would naturally wonder what could open up a location to this sort of chaos. Cranmer's case centers on the purported work of an abortion doctor and the murder of a family as the catalyst. And McEntire said he believes occult activity is a common cause of infestation.

"A site that's been used for pagan worship is another one," he said. "At the same time, if you're dealing with a location that, let's say is commonly used for drug deals, I would fully expect there to be something lingering around in that place." He added that it's a good idea to "pray through" locations such as hotel rooms, as the activities that unfold there could open doors for spiritual issues to linger.

As for specific solutions to the sorts of problems that come from purported infestation, McEntire said there are fixes that range from uttering simple blessings to specified prayers—to tactics that are more sweeping. "For those from sacramental backgrounds, such as Anglican and Orthodox, celebrating the Eucharist on that location can also be a key breaking point in the demonic hold of the place," he said.

Many pastors and theologians agree that one of the common mistakes people make when they suspect spiritual issues in their homes is to turn to ghost hunters, psychics, and other perceived spiritual experts. McEntire openly warned against this approach. "Many of the people who get involved in that actually do have a background in the occult and it can actually strengthen the spirit's hold in the place," he said.

McEntire's opinions are certainly food for thought, and there are countless stories that mirror Cranmer's purported experience.

The stories of Robbie, the Ammons family, and Cranmer are three collective claims of the demonic among a sea of other such stories, and they warrant some deeper understanding of what exorcisms, deliverance, and spiritual remedy truly look like.

Regardless of where people stand on these purported spiritual struggles, some important questions must be raised: How are these phenomena dealt with in our modern world, and who are the people who engage in such activities?

But before we get there, perhaps there's a more pressing curiosity: What does the Bible say about these spiritual subjects?

PART TWO

WHAT THE BIBLE SAYS

4

Satan's Nature and Impact

Satan is a powerful, potent . . . force in our lives, as are his minions." Bible teacher Hank Hanegraaff didn't mince words as he described his views on the devil's impact over our lives, noting that spiritual warfare is really "the battle for the mind."

Hanegraaff said it's as though Satan sits on our shoulders and whispers into our ear, attempting to tweak or transform our thoughts.

"The whisper cannot be heard with the physical ear, but it does penetrate the ear of the mind," Hanegraaff said. "And therefore the battle for the mind is a battle against the intrusive thoughts, anxious worries, and idle concerns that Satan foists upon us."

These ideas aren't merely human inventions or whims, and Hanegraaff is hardly the first to promulgate them. In fact, the Bible has much to say about Satan's nature as well as his impact on our world.

Despite contemporary culture's penchant for shying away from conversations about demonic influence, the Scriptures make it clear that there is a spiritual battle between good and evil that has been raging beneath our material surface since Satan's fall.

The Bible frames it as a diabolical struggle that cannot be seen by the human eye, but that can, at times, be palpably felt and experienced through the harrowing events that unfold in our individual and collective lives. But what can we know about this struggle? For the Christian, the Bible serves as the baseline, offering truths intended to help believers understand the essential elements of life and spiritual practice.

> *Scriptures make it clear that there is a spiritual battle between good and evil that has been raging beneath our material surface since Satan's fall.*

It is there, in the Scriptures, that the nature of these evils can be understood. Ephesians 6 offers some startling descriptions of what the Bible claims is unfolding in the spiritual realm, as the text encourages humans to "put on the full armor of God" so that we can "stand against the devil's schemes" (v. 11).

These references are revealing in that they drive home some important points about the Christian worldview: there is a cunning enemy who has the ability to mislead us, but God gives us the power to ward off the devil's diabolical forces.

"The Bible tells us that we are in a battle with Satan himself," Dr. Michael Brown told me in an interview for this book. "The Bible tells us that we're not wrestling with flesh and blood, but with demonic powers operating in a systematic, coordinated way. So to be sober-minded means to recognize the reality of the spiritual realm."

We see this dynamic being explained in the biblical text, as there is a stirring description of the darkness unfolding beneath the surface—a dynamic that often bubbles over to the world around us, and one that should, from a biblical sense, cause us to draw closer to God.

"For our struggle is not against flesh and blood, but against the rulers, against the authorities, against the powers of this dark world and against the spiritual forces of evil in the heavenly realms,"

Ephesians 6:12 reads, with verse 13 continuing, "Therefore put on the full armor of God, so that when the day of evil comes, you may be able to stand your ground, and after you have done everything, to stand."

It is with the "shield of faith" that we can "extinguish all the flaming arrows of the evil one" (v. 16). There's a lot there to unpack, but even the most ardent critic would do well to try and understand what, from a Christian perspective, the Bible is affirming. The idea that there are demonic and diabolical forces at work—influences that we cannot see but that have a direct impact on everything from our personal decisions to our social and political movements—is nothing new. And Ephesians 6 seems to capture that dynamic while also simultaneously offering a warning to every person who claims to believe in the Almighty: be on guard.

All of this boils down to the need to understand, from a biblical perspective, the character of Satan and his role not only in human history but also in contemporary matters. As Brown told me, the Bible paints Satan as "a murderer and a liar" who is in total rebellion against God, and that description alone is incredibly instructive.

"There's nothing good about him and . . . his goal is to destroy human beings. His goal is to defile the name of God. His goal is to present us something that looks so good, but in the end is absolute death," Brown said. "He is associated with everything on the wrong side, with darkness, with death, with evil, with hatred, with lies, with violence. This is who he is. This is what motivates him and moves him."

Brown, who summarized Satan as being both "diabolical and extreme," added that he believes the devil's most pervasive method for attacking God is to target human beings to try and separate us from the Lord. "*Diabolical* is the word from which we get devil," Brown said. "And he is clever and he is cunning and he is relentless with an army of demons out to destroy."

We can look to the Bible's narrative, filled with centuries-old claims about Satan and his nature, to better understand what Christianity teaches about the devil.

Satan's Roots

Satan is described as behaving in a number of pervasive ways throughout Scripture, with various stories and descriptions offering a human lens into his fiendish nature. Some Bible experts see notable differences when it comes to how Satan is presented in the Old and New Testaments. Dr. Shane Wood cautions that there's not a great multitude of information about the devil in the Old Testament—at least not as much as one might expect. He said satanology in the Old Testament is "actually shockingly absent."

"It's not robust. I mean, you see it. . . . You see it in spurts, sometimes dramatically, like in Job where chapters 1 and 2 offer a very unique moment of Satan even dialoguing with God," he said. "But in the Old Testament, you just don't get much."

Wood said that there were some key developments in the understanding of Satan during the roughly four-hundred-year gap between the writing of Malachi and Matthew. During this time, Jewish (intertestamental) literature seemed to dive deeper into these themes.

"In your intertestamental literature from the four-hundred-year gap between the Old and New Testament, you have some pretty clear developments of angelology, and even demonology and satanology," he said. "Now, once we get to the New Testament, the Satan figure is a lot more solidified."

Wood was careful to note that this trajectory is not an example of any sort of evolution of truth or fabrication of reality, but that it, instead, indicates that truth was increasingly being revealed and understood by humans as time progressed. "I don't believe that this is just a mythology that's grown just to a more lucid form in the New Testament," he said. "I believe it's revelation."

Indiana-based pastor and author Lucas Miles essentially echoed these sentiments and pointed to an important dynamic that people must consider when attempting to understand Christianity: the source of some of the most popular details surrounding Satan. "We have to first recognize that the majority of what we think we know about Satan and the demonic and demonic oppression, it comes more from church history, from books like Milton's *Paradise Lost* or *Dante's Inferno*, than it does actually from Scripture," he said. "Much of what is sort of propagated is really just tradition, rather than based upon biblical scholarship, or even biblical study at a devotional level."

From a comprehensive and data-driven standpoint, these proclamations should matter to Christians and non-Christians alike, especially if an accurate theological depiction of evil is to be understood. Rather than taking cues from books, movies, and culture, these experts would note that we must dive into Scripture to understand what we can definitely know about the devil.

To begin, the Bible tells us that Satan is a deceiver and liar who routinely authors, sparks, and perpetuates confusion. Revelation 12:9 tells us that Satan "leads the whole world astray," and 1 John 3:8 proclaims that "the devil has been sinning from the beginning," going on to note that Jesus came to "destroy the devil's work."

Here are some of the other places where we get a sense of Satan's diabolical character:

- The devil is an "enemy" who "prowls around like a roaring lion" (1 Peter 5:8).
- Satan hatches "schemes" (Ephesians 6:11).
- He is a "tempter" (Matthew 4:3 and 1 Thessalonians 3:5).
- Satan is the "prince of this world" (John 12:31).

- The devil is a deceiver who has "blinded the minds of unbelievers" (2 Corinthians 4:4).
- He is at work "in those who are disobedient" (Ephesians 2:2).
- Satan is an "accuser" (Revelation 12:10).

It's noteworthy that John tells us that the devil's schemes started at the "beginning," and it takes just three chapters at the start of Genesis for us to see the devil fast at work deceiving, sparking confusion, and negatively influencing humanity. We learn in Genesis 2 that God put Adam in the garden of Eden, telling Adam and Eve that they were free to eat from any tree so long as they did not take food from the tree of the knowledge of good and evil. God warned that the duo would "certainly die" if they defied this order (v. 17).

Most of us know how the story goes, with Adam and Eve being deceived by the devil, who appears as a serpent (interestingly, Revelation 12 also refers to Satan as an "ancient serpent called the devil" [v. 9]). It's the serpent that led them into temptation and, in turn, catapulted humanity into sin.

Genesis 3 describes the serpent as "more crafty than any of the wild animals the LORD God had made" (v. 1). The dialogue between Satan and Eve before the fall of man is also quite telling, as we see the devil questioning Eve about God's rule that she and Adam refrain from eating the forbidden fruit. "Did God really say, 'You must not eat from any tree in the garden'?" Satan asked.

The question itself is incredibly deceptive, with trap-setting embedded in its very formation. Eve explained that she and Adam were free to eat from the trees in the garden, but that they were not permitted to eat from the tree of the knowledge of good and evil.

It is here that Satan's manipulation fully takes form, as he told Eve she would not "certainly die" and proceeded to place an idea in her head: that she and Adam could actually be like God. Ironically, it is this very idea—the notion that people are the arbiters of their own lives and destinies and that we get to decide what is right, wrong, and permissible—that has plagued humanity since the dawn of creation. This weakness of wanting to be like the Lord is something Satan preyed upon, as he manipulated truth to birth an amalgam of intrigue and bewilderment.

"For God knows that when you eat from it your eyes will be opened, and you will be like God, knowing good and evil," the serpent responded (Genesis 3:5). And that was all it took. Eve suddenly saw the untouchable food as pleasing and "desirable for gaining wisdom" (v. 6), so she ate it and gave it to Adam, who also consumed it.

The Bible tells us that this act—bred from and rooted in the deception of Satan—transformed the human race and set creation on course to need a redeemer.

Regardless of what people believe about the aforementioned narrative, the story describes humanity's first interaction with Satan, and it exposes how people tend to act when caught doing something unpalatable or sinful. When you read the text, there is a bit of a blame game that goes on in the garden once God found out that Adam and Eve failed to heed his command, with Adam affirming that Eve gave him the food and Eve proclaiming, "The serpent deceived me" (v. 13).

From there, the rest is history. Adam and Eve were banished from the garden, and the trajectory of the human experience dramatically changed. This is just one of the most essential biblical stories we can read to better understand Satan's diabolical nature.

SATAN ACCUSES JOB

John called Satan an "accuser" (Revelation 12:10), which is a notable descriptor, especially when we examine Job's story in the Old Testament. It's one of the Bible's most well-known narratives, with much of the attention focusing on Job's reactions to the horrific events that befell him and his family.

It's also a confusing story on the surface, sparking a plethora of questions about God, goodness, pain, suffering, and the role and power of good and evil in our lives. The Bible Project perhaps most astutely summarized Job when it described the book as "one of the most sophisticated and mind-bending literary works in the Bible."[1]

Among the many themes and happenings, Satan's role in the story is noteworthy, with the devil appearing just six verses into the first chapter of the book. Before Satan's arrival, we learn that Job lived in a place called Uz and was "blameless and upright." We are also told that he "feared God and shunned evil," and, according to the biblical text, he became a target for Satan to accuse before God (Job 1:1).

Job 1:6–7 offers a fascinating scenario in which angels came before God and "Satan also came with them." God asked the devil, "Where have you come from?" to which Satan replied, "From roaming throughout the earth, going back and forth on it."

From there, God mentioned Job and emphasized his goodness, faithfulness, and unique nature, stating that there was no one like him on the Earth. That's when Satan began to accuse, appealing to rhetorical questions about Job and alleging that Job would "curse" God if the good in his life were stripped away (v. 11).

"Does Job fear God for nothing? . . . Have you not put a hedge around him and his household and everything he has?" Satan proclaimed. "You have blessed the work of his hands, so that his flocks and herds are spread throughout the land. But now stretch out your hand and strike everything he has, and he will surely curse you to your face" (vv. 9–11).

The Bible Project summarizes Satan's proclamations as follows:

Isn't it possible that Job's virtuous behavior is motivated by selfishness? If Job knows that good behavior brings divine blessing and abundance, then he could have all kinds of reasons for being "blameless and upright." If that were the case, then Job's goodness isn't really that good, and even more importantly, it calls into question God's basic policy of rewarding those who honor and follow him.[2]

These accusations have quite a bit of depth. It is unclear why, but God allowed Satan to have authority over "everything [Job] has," though the devil was commanded not to harm Job (v. 12).

Most people know what happened next. Job lost his servants and sheep in an attack and fire, his camels were taken, and his sons and daughters were killed. But though Satan accused him before God, the Bible tells us that "Job did not sin by charging God with wrongdoing" (v. 22).

Satan, being a diabolical accuser, was not satisfied with Job's reaction, so we see him once again approaching God, with the Lord praising Job's integrity despite all that befell him. The devil told God, though, that he believed Job would curse the Lord if God allowed Job to suffer physically and not just through material and familial losses.

"Skin for skin! . . . A man will give all he has for his own life," Satan said in Job 2:4, continuing in verse 5, "But now stretch out your hand and strike his flesh and bones, and he will surely curse you to your face."

God allowed Satan to test this theory but told him to spare Job's life. Satan promptly afflicted Job with "painful sores from the soles of his feet to the crown of his head" (v. 7). As a result, Job questioned the Lord and learned a great many lessons. Despite his suffering, he recognized "his need to totally trust" in God and was "restored to health, happiness and prosperity beyond his earlier state," as GotQuestions.org notes.[3]

One of the most fascinating takeaways from this story is that sin is not always the catalyst for our struggles and that God is always there for us, regardless of what unfolds.

SATAN'S ATTEMPTS TO SWAY CHRIST

Another key biblical story that offers us a true lens into the devil's schemes comes when we see him repeatedly confronting and testing Jesus in the wilderness, a narrative that is mentioned and explained in Mark, Luke, and Matthew.

Mark 1 tells us that Jesus was baptized by John the Baptist in Galilee and the Spirit immediately "sent him out into the wilderness" (v. 12). The text notes that he was there "forty days, being tempted by Satan" (v. 13).

As the story is recounted in Matthew and Luke, we see the devil once again attempt to sway someone, only this time Satan was dealing with history's only truly sinless person, as the Bible tells us, "For in Christ all the fullness of the Deity lives in bodily form" (Colossians 2:9). It is worth noting that Satan came to Jesus when Christ had been fasting for forty days and forty nights, as Luke tells us that Christ "ate nothing" during that time (Luke 4:2).

One can imagine the level of starvation Jesus might have been experiencing at that point, so it is not a detail to be lost on the reader. Without a doubt, the devil was intentionally preying on the circumstances in Jesus' life. Seizing a weak moment to try and capitalize on Jesus' vulnerability, he began imploring Christ to turn stones into bread.

"If you are the Son of God, tell these stones to become bread," Satan proclaimed (Matthew 4:3). Jesus responded by proclaiming, "It is written: 'Man shall not live on bread alone, but on every word that comes from the mouth of God'" (v. 4).

Christ was quoting from Deuteronomy 8:3 while delivering a powerful rebuke of Satan's words. But the Bible tells us the devil wasn't done there, as he took Jesus to Jerusalem and brought him to the highest point of the temple. It is here that Satan quoted Psalm 91:11–12 as he interacted with Jesus—a notable moment that affirmed the devil's knowledge of the biblical narrative.

"If you are the Son of God, . . . throw yourself down," Satan told Jesus. "For it is written: 'He will command his angels concerning you, and they will lift you up in their hands, so that you will not strike your foot against a stone'" (Matthew 4:6).

Jesus again responded to Satan with scripture, noting the Bible's proclamations in Deuteronomy 6:16. Christ said, "It is also written: 'Do not put the Lord your God to the test'" (Matthew 4:7). This back and forth culminated with Satan taking Christ to a "very high mountain"—a location that allowed the devil to show Jesus "all the kingdoms of the world and their splendor" (v. 8).

It was here that Satan directly attempted to get Jesus to worship him, promising Christ authority over all that was before them. "All this I will give you, if you will bow down and worship me," Satan said (v. 9).

Jesus, of course, responded with a rebuke rooted in Scripture (words that can be found in Deuteronomy 6:13), proclaiming, "Away from me, Satan!" before adding, "For it is written: 'Worship the Lord your God, and serve him only'" (Matthew 4:10).

The Bible tells us that Satan left Jesus and that the angels came to attend to Christ. Anyone who understands the scope and trajectory of the Christian scriptures understands why Jesus would have never fallen to Satan's schemes, though the lesson here is profound: we, as humans, are vulnerable and must be on guard.

SATAN IN THE GOSPELS: A RECAP

It is clear that Satan makes a pointed appearance in the Gospels, with these stories shedding light on his nature. At other points in

Scripture, we see Jesus offering additional details about the devil, including Christ's proclamation in Luke 10 that he saw Satan fall from heaven.

Jesus' revelation comes after he sent seventy-two disciples out, two by two, to every town and location he planned to visit. These individuals returned to Jesus and were filled with joy, proclaiming, "Lord, even the demons submit to us in your name" (Luke 10:17).

"I saw Satan fall like lightning from heaven. I have given you authority to trample on snakes and scorpions and to overcome all the power of the enemy; nothing will harm you," Jesus said, and then delivered a line of caution. "However, do not rejoice that the spirits submit to you, but rejoice that your names are written in heaven" (vv. 18–20).

Jesus' area of focus here is thought provoking, as he noted his authority and, in turn, the power he had given to the disciples. But rather than focus on that power, he encouraged them to rejoice that they will inherit salvation. This coincides with Jesus' earlier dismissal of the devil and his power to avoid and dissuade evil; it is a function that, from a biblical perspective, is also available to Christians.

Christ's refusal to listen to Satan as well as his demand that the devil leave him offer powerful, collective examples and profound insights for humans. We see these themes in other areas of Scripture, with James, Jesus' brother, imploring Christians to submit themselves to God.

"Resist the devil," he wrote, "and he will flee from you" (James 4:7).

There is similar language in 1 Peter 5, warning that Christians must guard their hearts and minds, with the devil being presented as an animal seeking to seize people's weakest moments.

"Be alert and of sober mind. Your enemy the devil prowls around like a roaring lion looking for someone to devour," verse 8 reads, with verse 9 continuing, "Resist him, standing firm in the faith, because you know that the family of believers throughout the world is undergoing the same kind of sufferings."

The Scriptures promise in other areas that God will protect those seeking to push back against Satan or to avoid his attacks, with 2 Thessalonians 3:3 proclaiming that God is "faithful" and will "strengthen you and protect you from the evil one."

The entire story arc of human existence and God's decision to send a Savior coincide with this promised protection that is seen in the Scriptures.

"Instead of taking out his wrath on us, God became a man, and then equally poured out his wrath upon Lucifer and mankind in the person of Jesus on the cross, so that we can now have authority over the oppression of the enemy," pastor Lucas Miles said, "and be able to walk in authority as a believer, and be able to see healing take place and operate in the Spirit and all these things that happen."

This brings us full circle back to Ephesians 6:10–17, which, again, speaks to the power that can be found in putting on "the full armor of God" in an effort to "take your stand against the devil's schemes" (v. 11). Verses 12–17 offer some truly profound words that are worth presenting here:

> For our struggle is not against flesh and blood, but against the rulers, against the authorities, against the powers of this dark world and against the spiritual forces of evil in the heavenly realms. Therefore put on the full armor of God, so that when the day of evil comes, you may be able to stand your ground, and after you have done everything, to stand. Stand firm then, with the belt of truth buckled around your waist, with the breastplate of righteousness in place, and with your feet fitted with the readiness that comes from the gospel of peace. In addition to all this, take up the shield of faith, with which you can extinguish all the flaming

arrows of the evil one. Take the helmet of salvation and the sword
of the Spirit, which is the word of God.

Part of understanding what the Bible says about these themes is
recognizing the impact of evil in our hearts and on our world.

Hanegraaff noted that Satan and his minions seek to "undo us
by thoughts," putting ideas into our minds that we might not even
realize are not our own ideas and whims.

While Satan cannot read our minds, he can influence our thoughts.
Thus, the Bible instructs us to "put on the full armor of God so that
you can take your stand against the devil's schemes." Without it,
you are a guaranteed casualty in the invisible war; with it, you are
invincible. If we open the door to Satan by failing to put on the full
armor of God, he does, as it were, sit on our shoulders and whisper
into our ears. The whisper cannot be discerned with the physical
ear; it can, however, penetrate 'the ear' of the mind.

Many Christian pastors and theologians will warn that there is
a danger in placing too much emphasis and blame on Satan and not
enough on human free will, though these experts will also note that dismissing the former does not mesh well with what we see in Scripture.

"We have to recognize that, yes, what we human beings do, we
are responsible for," Dr. Michael Brown said. "But when you see certain things so evil, so dark, so sick, so demented, and then when
people talk about they just were under control of some other being
or they did things they can't imagine they would ever do, you have
to recognize the hand of Satan in this as well."

Brown said it is scary to see "how easy it is to be drawn to dark
things" as human beings, but he spoke of the importance of seeking
healing and powerful protection. "That's why we need grace," Brown
said. "That's why we need the Lord Jesus."

For his part, Hanegraaff said we can push back against Satan by training ourselves to "cut off the intrusive thoughts"—something we can accomplish through Christ.

"The power of God to protect is greater than the power of Satan to pillage," he said. "So, the emphasis on spiritual warfare is always on the provision that God has given to us to stand firm and after everything, to stand—to stand against principalities and powers of darkness."

Understanding the "powers of darkness" through a biblical lens is relatively simple, though some theological debates have broken out when it comes to the nature of the demons said to help Satan fulfill his mission on Earth.

5

WHAT DEMONS ARE

If a person entertains the existence of demons, he or she is then naturally faced with the task of understanding the nature of these beings: where they originated, what they are, how they can manifest, and what gives them "legal rights" to appear in the physical realm.

These curiosities obviously mean nothing to someone who outright dismisses their existence, but any Christian—even a person who believes that demons and possession are no longer part of our natural world or were confined to biblical times—must confront the reality of these figures' existence and manifestation.

This can be a profound challenge and quest. After all, biblical encounters with the demonic are described as being palpably real and anything but symbolic, yet, through today's materialist lens, the topic sometimes feels strange or disconnected from our daily reality.

"I think people just enjoy ignorance on this more than truth," Chad Norris, senior pastor at Bridgeway Church in Greenville, South Carolina, told me. And he makes a solid point. For many reasons, some Christians simply avoid or ignore these stories and realities, tucking them away as vestiges of a past biblical era or as current realities they would simply rather not confront.

But for any professed Christian to dismiss demons as mere works of fiction—forces that have never truly existed—would seem strange, problematic, and a spiritual slope so slippery that it would undoubtedly call into question every other element of Scripture. After all, one cannot embrace some elements of the Bible as true and others as false and still claim reliability of the Scriptures.

When we read what the Bible has to say about various possessions, it seems we are each faced with a choice: either the Scriptures are conjuring up themes and happenings that never unfolded—the biblical writers are exclusively mistaking mental illness for something spiritual—or the demonic realm is one that exists and, in turn, must be concretely understood.

Just how pervasive are these themes in the Bible? The New Testament mentions the term "unclean spirits"—wording that refers to the demonic—twenty-five times, with demons being mentioned an additional twenty-nine times throughout those texts.[1] Most specifically, Jesus' exorcisms are among these references that appear throughout the biblical text and, as we will explore in this book, are far from symbolic moments or mere bouts with benign spiritual struggle.

These encounters were radical healings in which the Bible alleges that Christ expelled demonic forces from having what appears to be total control over children and adults alike. The stories we read in the Bible showcase the dangerous, potentially deadly, and tragic impact that possession can have over the lives of those impacted.

So, even if a person concludes that this was a phenomenon that exclusively existed during Jesus' earthly ministry, then those nagging questions still remain: What are demons and where did they originate?

"It might surprise a lot of people who are familiar with the

Bible . . . to know that the Bible never offers a point-blank explanation for where demons come from," Dr. Michael Heiser told me in a 2015 interview on the topic. "A lot of what we think about that is really filtered through church tradition."[2]

As it turns out, theologians and pastors have divergent ideas when it comes to answering this key question, though the baseline interpretation is that demons are diabolical entities that are depraved and fallen in nature—a detail the biblical texts and many contemporary experts seem to agree on.

"[Demons are] fallen entities that were once part of the collective, of a celestial collective that worshiped the land, that worshiped God, and [they were] rebellious of course," Reverend Sam Rodriguez told me.

Most theologians describe demons as being overtaken by darkness with a disconnect from God so pronounced that their antics are unimaginably evil in nature. All of this is based on the decision to separate from their Creator and to align with Satan, whose attributes we've already covered in detail.

"I believe that what demons are, are intelligent entities that are willfully moving away from God as their center," Dr. Shane Wood said, affirming this position.

But when it comes to their deeper nature, there is a bit of divide. Some take definitive positions on various theories, while others are incredibly cautious surrounding how they approach the topic and what, exactly, they are willing to publicly settle on.

"So, what do I think demons are? Truthfully, I don't know that I know," Wood said. "Is it possible that they're fallen angels? I actually have evidence that [some] angels are against God in the Bible. There are certain ones that are, so I'm not against that."

Wood does reject the idea that demons are people's spirits after death, though, proclaiming that he does not see evidence for this dynamic in Scripture; and as we will see later on in the chapter, he acknowledges the existence of another theological theory: that demons are actually something the Bible refers to as "Nephilim."

Pulling back a bit, there are some simple facts we can take away from the Bible surrounding the spiritual nature of demons and the ways in which they can manifest. Regardless of whether one approaches the topic of demonic possession as an atheist, a Christian, or anything in between, the Scriptures make it clear that these beings are spirits that can take control of people's bodies and lives.

Dr. David Jeremiah, pastor of Shadow Mountain Community Church in El Cajon, California, has noted that "spirits do not have physical bodies, but they can inhabit a body" and emphasized that it's possible for "multiple spirits to possess the same body," as biblical stories illustrate.[3]

Fallen Angels as Demons

The most common theological understanding is that demons are "fallen angels" who have chosen to turn against God. Dr. Jeremiah holds to this view, pointing to Revelation 12 as offering "hints" surrounding how angels fell and essentially became the demonic forces we see in Scripture.

"Revelation 12 hints that a third of heaven's angels fell from God's grace when Lucifer became Satan," he wrote on his website. "These fallen angels are also called demons. Some of them sinned so gravely that God has already imprisoned them in hell. Others remain free, working to disrupt God's plan and distract people from God's truth."[4]

It's important to note that the reference about angels falling from heaven and becoming demons is based on a specific interpretation of Revelation 12:4. In the preceding verse, there is a description of an "an enormous red dragon with seven heads and ten horns and seven crowns on its heads."

Verse 4 tells us: "Its tail swept a third of the stars out of the sky and flung them to the earth. The dragon stood in front of the woman who was about to give birth, so that it might devour her child the moment he was born."

This text obviously does not use direct language that speaks of angels or demons, but the Christian Apologetics and Research Ministry (CARM) explains that there is a baseline from which this interpretation is reached.[5] According to CARM, angels are often referred to symbolically in Jewish literature as stars—something that CARM noted happens in Revelation 1:20.[6] That verse, which refers to Jesus' revelation to John, reads:

> The mystery of the seven stars that you saw in my right hand and
> of the seven golden lampstands is this: The seven stars are the
> angels of the seven churches, and the seven lampstands are the
> seven churches.

This belief in demons' nature is intriguing for a plethora of reasons. At the center of the discussion is the idea that angels themselves have free will—the ability to choose right and wrong and, invariably, the ability to accept or reject God and Christ.

"In a biblical worldview, what you have is you have God creating angels, but God creates those angels with libertarian freedom. They have freedom to act or to act otherwise," famed author and Bible teacher Hank Hanegraaff—a former evangelical who joined the Eastern Orthodox Church in 2017—told me. "He doesn't create them so that they have to worship him, but they worship him of their own volition."

He continued, "You have in the biblical narrative, a fall of Satan, and Satan takes a third of the angels with him in that fall. In other words, a third of the angels of their own volition, of their own free choice, seek to follow the Prince of Darkness rather than the Prince of Light."

We see in the book of Jude some truly thought-provoking claims about angels that seem to corroborate the idea that they have (or at least at one point had) the free choice to either remain with God or choose to abandon him. Jude wrote about corrupt people who were intermingling with believers and warned that these individuals were "ungodly people, who pervert the grace of our God into a license for immorality and deny Jesus Christ our only Sovereign and Lord" (Jude 1:4).

He then noted that God delivered his people from Egypt, but "destroyed those who did not believe" (v. 5). It is what comes next in verses 6–7, though, that gives us some insight into what the Bible teaches about angels:

> And the angels who did not keep their positions of authority but abandoned their proper dwelling—these he has kept in darkness, bound with everlasting chains for judgment on the great Day. In a similar way, Sodom and Gomorrah and the surrounding towns gave themselves up to sexual immorality and perversion. They serve as an example of those who suffer the punishment of eternal fire.

The use of the past tense when it comes to angels' decisions not to follow God is thought provoking. This begs the question: Could or would an angel still have the ability to reject God, or was it something that happened at a fixed point in time?

One can go down a bit of a rabbit hole in an attempt to explore these theological considerations, so we will not devote too much time to this specific topic, though it is worth noting that there are some scholars who believe that the event described in Jude 1 was essentially a "probation period" similar to the time Adam and Eve lived in the garden.[7]

Under this worldview, the angels chose at a past, fixed point in time to either accept or reject God, with those who chose rejection joining Satan and the majority remaining with God. Some see the biblical description of angels as "holy" as something that should give us pause when considering whether angels might still decide to turn from God.

Jesus mentioned "holy angels" in Mark 8:38 when he proclaimed, "If anyone is ashamed of me and my words in this adulterous and sinful generation, the Son of Man will be ashamed of them when he comes in his Father's glory with the holy angels" (similar language is used in Psalm 89:5).[8]

Considering the gravity of the world *holy*—a descriptor that is also given to Christ—the assumption here is that, though the angels that remain with God still technically have the ability to sin, they likely will not. GotQuestions.org compared this dynamic to Jesus' own story; Christ was tempted and had the ability to choose but never fell to sin.[9]

This latter debate aside, the main point to take away from this discussion is that many Christian pastors and theologians believe that fallen angels who chose to embrace the devil became demons and have been deceiving and tricking mankind since humanity's inception.[10]

THE OTHER THEORY SURROUNDING THE DEMONIC

Not everyone believes in the fallen-angel paradigm, with some positing other theories surrounding the nature and origins of demons. A group known as the Nephilim are mentioned by name twice in the Bible: in Genesis and Numbers. Genesis 6 offers a brief description of these mysterious figures—one that is presented just before the start of Noah's story.

We learn that there was intense wickedness in the world after

God created human beings. We also get some intriguing descriptions in Genesis 6:1–4 that might leave us with more questions than they do answers. Let's briefly explore the text in question:

> When human beings began to increase in number on the earth and daughters were born to them, the sons of God saw that the daughters of humans were beautiful, and they married any of them they chose. Then the LORD said, "My Spirit will not contend with humans forever, for they are mortal; their days will be a hundred and twenty years."
>
> The Nephilim were on the earth in those days—and also afterward—when the sons of God went to the daughters of humans and had children by them. They were the heroes of old, men of renown.

These lines of Scripture have sparked quite a bit of theological debate. As Dr. Jeremiah noted, "Scripture doesn't reveal many details about the Nephilim."

And Wood also discussed some of the strange elements surrounding these verses, specifically the term "sons of God," which he said was "around that time almost consistently 'angels.'" When one takes this into account and reads for context, even more questions emerge.

"So, that makes it even more strange how these angels are lusting after women and then the possibility of these offspring being Nephilim, but then it drops out of the Bible until Numbers 13," he said. And in Numbers 13:33 and Ezekiel 32:27, even fewer details are given.

Outside of these scripture references, the biblical text is largely silent about these Nephilim figures, which is why some theologians and pastors have declined to definitively dive deep into a subject that Scripture does not robustly contend with. Still, this has not stopped other pastors and theologians from theorizing that the Nephilim—and not fallen angels—are actually the main source of demonic activity.

While the Bible is largely silent about the Nephilim, there is another text used by some to derive details and claims about these figures—informational tidbits that serve as the underpinnings of demonic theory: 1 Enoch (also known as the book of Enoch).

"Chapters 1 through 36 of 1 Enoch is the book of the watchers where we get this . . . elaboration of the Nephilim," Wood said. "A lot of it's read back into the Old Testament. It's not necessarily that the Old Testament is arguing it, because whenever you read Genesis 6:1–4 . . . it is ambiguous."

From a Christian perspective, there are some notable problems with taking 1 Enoch at face value and using its contents to craft theological theories. Do not feel silly if you cannot find the book of Enoch in your Bible; it has never been a part of the biblical canon, as it is pseudepigraphal, which means that it is not included in any biblical canon and is falsely ascribed or attributed.[11]

That said, you will find Enoch in the Bible. He was the great-great-great-great-grandson of Adam, and the great-grandfather of Noah (you can read about the complete lineage in Genesis 5).[12] Here's what Genesis 5:21–24 tells us:

> When Enoch had lived 65 years, he became the father of Methuselah. After he became the father of Methuselah, Enoch walked faithfully with God 300 years and had other sons and daughters. Altogether, Enoch lived a total of 365 years. Enoch walked faithfully with God; then he was no more, because God took him away.

Despite the fact that Enoch is mentioned a number of places in Scripture, there are some serious conundrums surrounding the book of Enoch. Among them, it appears to have had multiple authors and cannot actually be traced back to Enoch. That said, while the book has never been considered reliable enough to be part of the canon, it did have an impact among Jews and early Christians.

"The Book of Enoch . . . was greatly revered among early Jews—First, Second century Jews—and even right before that, and the early followers of Jesus," Dr. Michael Brown has explained when speaking about this text.[13] "It was held in high esteem, but it was never considered to be part of the canon of scripture in any universal way."

Brown continued, "In other words, it did not have the divine stamp on it saying that this is a book that should be part of the canon of scripture and therefore was embraced by the community of believers as being authentically scripture."[14]

If anyone is looking for evidence that early Christians not only had knowledge of the book of Enoch but were also deeply intrigued by its contents, look no further than Jude, Jesus' brother and the author of the book of Jude in the New Testament. Just a few verses after Jude wrote about angels abandoning their place of authority, he quoted from Enoch.

> Enoch, the seventh from Adam, prophesied about them: "See, the Lord is coming with thousands upon thousands of his holy ones to judge everyone, and to convict all of them of all the ungodly acts they have committed in their ungodliness, and of all the defiant words ungodly sinners have spoken against him." These people are grumblers and faultfinders; they follow their own evil desires; they boast about themselves and flatter others for their own advantage. (Jude 1:14–16)

Before we dive deeper into the Nephilim discussion, we must confront why someone like Jude would quote from the book of Enoch, and why that quote would make its way into Scripture—especially if the book of Enoch is not, itself, reliable enough to be considered a viable staple in the biblical canon.

Understandably, this has led some to posit that perhaps the book of Enoch should carry more biblical weight than it does; considering what this pseudepigraphal text says about demons and spiritual warfare, this is a point worthy of further exploration. Brown has noted that God clearly chose not to include the book of Enoch in the biblical canon and offered some important caveats worth considering surrounding Jude's use of Enoch.

"Just because something is quoted doesn't mean that it's all-inspired," he said. "It could just be one particular line that's being referenced as accurate or true or simply a point of reference."[15] One could conclude, as Brown noted, that it is entirely possible that Enoch's actual words were passed down through the generations and included in the book of Jude based on oral tradition. But using the very presence of Enoch's comments in the New Testament to justify the book of Enoch in its entirety is ideologically and theologically problematic.

"Enoch is certainly not the composer of the entire book, although perhaps some of his original sayings were preserved in it like what Jude quotes," Brown said. "But it's not part of the Bible because it was never intended by God to be part of the Bible."[16]

It should be noted that Jude also mentions a story about the archangel Michael disputing with the devil about the body of Moses that is retold in the Testament of Moses, yet another pseudepigraphical work mentioned by early church fathers but never included in the biblical text.

Paul, too, pointed to people outside of the Bible in Acts 17—a point that Wood used to illustrate that the book of Enoch isn't necessarily being endorsed but that the point being made in the specific reference is of note.

"Paul does that . . . with Greek poets and philosophers in

Acts 17," Wood said. "So, I don't know that it necessarily means that therefore 1 Enoch as a whole is inspired, but I do believe what it means is that Jude is looking at this particular text and saying, 'No, even non-canonical books have truth in them.'"

There is much discussion to be had surrounding these elements, though these explanations about the noncanonical texts are helpful to understanding why such statements and references would have made their way into Scripture.

WHAT ARE THE NEPHILIM?

With all of this in mind, let us revisit the Nephilim to better understand the arguments some make about their relation to the demonic realm. These figures have been described as "the product of the sons of god mingling with the daughters of Adam"[17] and Genesis 6:4 again calls them the "heroes of old, men of renown." These descriptions do not tell us much, though some proclaim that the name *Nephilim* itself translates to "fallen ones"[18] (others argue that it simply translates to "giants").[19]

What we do know does seem to point to these figures being giants and warriors. Dr. Ellen White explained some of the diverse theories surrounding the Nephilim, particularly the claim of their involvement in the events that sparked the great flood:

> It was once claimed that the mating of the sons of god and the daughters of Adam that resulted in the Nephilim caused the flood, and this caused the Nephilim to have a negative reputation. This was believed because the next verse (Genesis 6:5) is the introduction to the flood narrative and because their name means "fallen ones." It is unlikely that this interpretation is correct because Genesis 6:4 presents nothing but praise for the Nephilim and no

criticism is present. In addition, the name "fallen ones" is likely a reference to their divine paternity transforming—falling—into the human condition, albeit an almost superhuman condition.[20]

This brings us back to the book of Enoch, which deals with this theory on the flood, adding some new details and claims that are not found in the biblical text.[21]

In a brief explainer, Megan Sauter of the Biblical Archaeology Society tells us that the book of Enoch introduces the concept of the "Watchers"—"Fallen angels who mated with human women and produced offspring—the Nephilim, the 'heroes that were of old, warriors of renown' of Genesis 6:4—or giants."[22] This extra-biblical book indicates that the Watchers shared certain pieces of knowledge with their children and harmed the world, inserting intense evil throughout human existence.[23] In turn, these antics—at least according to the book of Enoch—sparked the flood.

You can see the origins of the Nephilim theory emerging in Enoch 6:1–3, which reads:

And it came to pass when the children of men had multiplied that in those days were born unto them beautiful and comely daughters. And the angels, the children of the heaven, saw and lusted after them, and said to one another: "Come, let us choose us wives from among the children of men and beget us children."[24]

In Enoch 7, we see this story intensify, with these angels taking wives and having "great giants" as children. The text claims that the situation soon turned problematic, with the giants turning against humans, with Enoch noting that they "devoured mankind" and "began to sin against birds, and beasts, and reptiles, and fish, and to devour one another's flesh, and drink the blood."[25]

One can see, then, how this narrative was used to justify the flood, but let's return to our original purpose: explaining the theory surrounding demonic possession and the Nephilim. Some theologians and Bible experts have contended that the spirits of the Nephilim became the demonic forces that many Christians believe are at work in our modern world.

"What the New Testament refers to as demons, Jewish texts in between the Old and New Testaments actually have a very clear answer for this—and that is demons are the disembodied spirits of the dead Nephilim from Genesis 6:1–4," Dr. Michael Heiser told me, "the dead giants of the pre-flood era and the post-flood era as well."[26]

It is a strange theory on the surface, and even well-respected theologians like Heiser admit that it "sounds kind of crazy," but the central idea behind this theory is that the Nephilim were once in bodily form but have been searching for new hosts since the great flood.[27]

Heiser has extensively written and spoken about the theory that "demons are the disembodied spirits of dead Nephilim giants who perished at the time of the great flood."[28] He and others who share his theological view on this matter believe that many Christian thinkers have missed the connections in Scripture that point to indications that the giants referenced in the Old Testament were evil in nature. Heister wrote:

Later in biblical history, during the days of Moses and Joshua, the Israelites ran into groups of very large warriors called Anakim. Numbers 13:32–33 tells us explicitly that the Anakim came from the Nephilim. The giant clans went by other names as well: Emim, Zamzummim, and Rephaim (Deut. 2–3). The wars of conquest for the land required the annihilation of these giant Anakim, which is why Joshua summed up the conquest this way: "There was none of the Anakim left in the land of the people of Israel. Only in Gaza, in Gath, and in Ashdod did some remain." Those were three

Philistine cities. Goliath would come from one of them (Gath) in the days of David (1 Samuel 17:4).

The key to understanding how these giants were perceived as demons in the biblical material—an idea that got a lot of focus in Jewish writings produced after the Old Testament—is the term Rephaim. In the Old Testament, the Rephaim are described as giant warlords (Deuteronomy 2:8–11; 3:1–11; Joshua 13:12), but also as frightening, sinister disembodied spirits ("the shades") in the Underworld, called Sheol in Hebrew (Isaiah 14:9; 26:14; Job 26:5). The disembodied spirits of these giants were therefore associated with the abode of the dead, something everyone feared, since everyone feared death.[29]

Much of this reads like a horror novel, though the arguments are worthy of highlighting. Before we conclude this discussion about the Nephilim, it is also worth mentioning some of the other elements in the book of Enoch that have potentially shaped this theory of the demonic realm. In Enoch 15, the giants are described as being from "spirits and flesh," with the text noting that they will now be called "evil spirits" and that "the earth shall be their dwelling." And the description of their evil nature does not end there:

> And the spirits of the giants afflict, oppress, destroy, attack, do battle, and work destruction on the earth, and cause trouble: they take no food, but nevertheless hunger and thirst, and cause offences. And these spirits shall rise up against the children of men and against the women, because they have proceeded from them.[30]

One could easily see how someone could read these bits of text and see their connection to the demonic, though one must, again, understand the theological reality that the book of Enoch is not part of the biblical canon. And some like Hanegraaff see the entire

Nephilim argument as being forced into the Scriptures rather than standing as a reality that is implicit in the text.

"This idea of demon-human hybrids and all that goes with it is an imposition on scripture rather than an extraction from scripture," he said.

Others like Norris appear a bit more willing to live in the realm of uncertainty when it comes to the exact nature of demons. When asked if he believes they are fallen angels or Nephilim, he answered candidly: "I have no idea."

Considering that demons' nature of origin has very little to do with their perceived actions in the modern realm, this response is fascinating and, on a deeper level, refreshing.

One could easily argue that the origin of demons is of lesser theological importance than understanding the impact these spiritual forces can have on individuals and culture at large.

With that in mind, one final note about the discussion surrounding demons centers on their abilities. Some stories involve purported details including items flying off of shelves, bruising suddenly appearing on people's bodies, and other such physical manifestations. Many of these claims rely on these spiritual beings having the ability to physically manifest outside of a person's body.

Hanegraaff, though, drew a distinction between demons' ability to possess nonbelievers and their capability to manifest or cause physical events to take form.

"In terms of physicality, can demons bite us? Can demons hit us over the head? The answer to that question would be, 'No,'" he told me. "And the reason is demons are not physical beings. They're spiritual beings and so spiritual warfare is essentially the battle for the mind."

Hanegraaff was careful to note that demon possession is "a very real thing" for which nonbelievers are at risk, but his differentiation on the ability to physically manifest is worth noting, particularly as there are numerous stories that seem to allege that demons have the ability to create physical chaos.

This is a smaller piece of the theological puzzle, but the ability to understand these subtle differences helps to better comprehend the broader debate.

While it's possible to speculate or get caught in the weeds, the Bible is clear surrounding some of the actions demons *are* able to take. In fact, numerous stories involving Jesus' exoricsms of adults and children alike showcase how people were tragically impacted by possession, and how Christ ultimately delivered hope and healing to the afflicted.

6

JESUS AND DEMONIC POSSESSION

The New Testament narrative tells the immensely beautiful story of Jesus coming to Earth to save and redeem mankind, ushering in grace and forgiveness and reconciling mankind to the Almighty—events believed by Christians to constitute the collective fulfillment of Messianic Old Testament prophecies.

Christ's sacrifice is the core and heartbeat of the Christian faith, with his birth, death, and resurrection offering a spiritual antidote in a sick and beleaguered world. Fully understanding that paradigm requires a proper comprehension of the broader scope of Scripture, including the context of both the Old and New Testaments.

We learn a great deal about Jesus' life and ministry throughout the New Testament narrative, but one of the most overlooked portions of Christ's work surrounds the riveting and dramatic moments in which he healed people of demonic possession.

> *One of the most overlooked portions of Christ's work surrounds the riveting and dramatic moments in which he healed people of demonic possession.*

71

Some might see these healings as the remnants of a distant culture that mistakenly mistook mental affliction for something more, others might see these stories as unfolding exclusively during ancient times before ceasing, and a third group sees these accounts as examples of the real-life spiritual dangers that rage under the surface of our material world.

Regardless of how people choose to view spiritual healings, the moments that Christ chose to expel demons are both glaring and prevalent in the biblical narrative. The prominence and frequency of these stories in the biblical narrative are not only undeniable, but experts like Pastor Chad Norris believe it's also incredibly convicting, especially when you consider the substantial portion of Jesus' healing that fell under the deliverance umbrella.

"Ignorance is bliss. Most Christians just want to go to heaven when they die and not have to deal with this stuff. But you read the Gospels, you read Acts, it's so far from our current experience," he told me. "When I realized that one-third of the Lord's stories were deliverance, it bothered me theologically because I said, 'Well why am I not doing it?' One-third of his healings are actually delivered from demons. That's a lot."

And when you look at the text of the New Testament Scriptures, it's hard to ignore Norris's conviction on the matter. Matthew 4:24 proclaims, "News about [Jesus] spread all over Syria, and people brought to him all who were ill with various diseases, those suffering severe pain, the demon-possessed, those having seizures, and the paralyzed; and he healed them."

This verse not only claims Jesus healed physical ailments and pains, but it goes further, differentiating these illnesses from "demon possession." And countless stories reiterate these points, going into various levels of detail to explain the who, what, and how of Christ's dealings with the demonic.

For the Christian who looks to the Bible as truth, these stories present some fascinating questions; taken at face value, they turn both atheism and the obsession with the material on their heads, requiring deeper thought and reflection about the lessons we can—and must—take away.

Paul told us that human beings are embroiled in a spiritual battle—an intangible tug-of-war between the forces of good and evil, with the latter waging battle against human hearts and minds. "For our struggle is not against flesh and blood, but against the rulers, against the authorities, against the powers of this dark world and against the spiritual forces of evil in the heavenly realms" (Ephesians 6:12).

> *Human beings are embroiled in a spiritual battle—an intangible tug-of-war between the forces of good and evil, with the latter waging battle against human hearts and minds.*

As we explore these biblical accounts and the ramifications of playing with spiritual fire, Dr. Michael Heiser makes an essential and thought-provoking point worth keeping in mind: the Bible doesn't necessarily give specific reasons why people become possessed.

"We don't have enough information in the New Testament to know why a person . . . was possessed," he said. "We're not really told their story. We're just sort of confronted with, well, here's where we wound up." With that in mind, let's explore how Jesus repeatedly confronted evil and delivered afflicted people of the demons that were actively impacting and destroying their lives.

JESUS RESCUES A MAN IN CAPERNAUM

In Mark 1 and Luke 4 we learn of a man in Capernaum whom Jesus saved from demonic possession. The incredible moment unfolded on the Sabbath when Jesus was teaching inside of the synagogue. As the people listened in awe, a man "possessed by an impure spirit" spoke out with some stirring questions for Christ (v. 23):

> "What do you want with us, Jesus of Nazareth? Have you come to destroy us? I know who you are—the Holy One of God!" (Mark 1:24)

These questions are noteworthy, as they indicate that these spirits knew exactly who Jesus was and were fearful of what he would do to them.

Mark 1:25 reveals how Christ responded, sternly telling the spirit to "be quiet" before following that up with another command: "Come out of him!" The spirit then shook the man "violently" and left him "with a shriek."

This conjures up some gripping imagery. And it's no surprise that the onlookers at the time were mesmerized by what unfolded before them. Their response is captured in Mark 1:27–28: "The people were all so amazed that they asked each other, 'What is this? A new teaching—and with authority! He even gives orders to impure spirits and they obey him.' News about him spread quickly over the whole region of Galilee."

It should also be noted that Mark 1:34 mentions other exorcisms that Jesus performed. Christ's power over these spirits is implicit in the biblical narrative, with Luke 4:41 blatantly noting that he not only expelled these demons but held the power to prevent them from speaking.

The scripture reads, "Moreover, demons came out of many people, shouting, 'You are the Son of God!' But he rebuked them and would not allow them to speak, because they knew he was the Messiah."

This is just one of the places in the New Testament where we see these spiritual events take place.

JESUS CASTS DEMONS INTO PIGS

One of the most intriguing exorcisms to unfold in the Scriptures is recounted in Mark 5, Luke 8, and Matthew 8, but let's start by looking at Matthew 8, as each chapter approaches the event from a different perspective.

The scene presented in this portion of Scripture, which was set in the region of the Gadarenes, is both tragic and riveting, as two demon-possessed men emerged from tombs and confront Jesus. The description of the men coming out of tombs carries with it a connotation of an unfortunate, zombie-like state, as the Scriptures tell us that they were wildly diabolical and "so violent that no one could pass that way" (Matthew 8:28).

Much like other demons we meet in Scripture, they, too, seemed petrified of Christ. "What do you want with us, Son of God?" they shouted (v. 29). "Have you come here to torture us before the appointed time?" Once again, the demons knew Jesus' identity, and they even seemed to know there was an "appointed time" that a reckoning will take place.

It's what happens next, though, that differentiates this event from the others. Subsequent verses don't attribute the speech that follows to the men, but to the evil spirits within them, noting that "the demons begged Jesus" (v. 31) to send them inside a nearby herd of pigs. This pleading reveals that they recognized his power to expel them yet were desperate for a new "host."

Interestingly, with the simple command of "Go!" Jesus agreed with the request, and the demons rushed out of the men and into the pigs—but that's not the end of the story. The pigs proceeded to run into a lake and then died in the water. As you can imagine, it was likely quite a sight to see, and it understandably left the people tending to the pigs so flabbergasted that they "went into the town and reported all this, including what had happened to the demon-possessed men" (v. 33). The people then came to Jesus and begged him to leave the area.

This story takes a slightly different form in both Mark 5 and Luke 8. Most notably, these chapters—which appear to be speaking of the same exorcism—mention only one demon-possessed man. And rather than the region of Gadarenes, Mark 5 and Luke 8 proclaim that the event unfolded in the area of Gerasenes (it's likely that this is the same area).

In this version of the account, "a man with an impure spirit" came out of the tombs and met Christ (Mark 5:2). Mark and Luke tell us that the man lived in the tombs—and Luke tells us that he hadn't worn clothes for a long time, shedding light on the tragic state of affairs. There are other additional details that can be found in Mark and Luke as well, particularly when it comes to the man's demeanor.

While the two men described in Matthew were unimaginably violent, new details emerge about the man in Mark that point to an even wilder nature. Mark tells us that chains couldn't even contain him and that he was able to tear apart and break irons used to hold his feet—pointing to the notion that he was experiencing a supernatural or extra-human level of strength.

In fact, Mark 5:4–5 tells us the extent of his bizarre behavior: "No one was strong enough to subdue him. Night and day among the tombs and in the hills he would cry out and cut himself with stones." Luke 8 proclaims that the demons drove the man into places of solitude. When Jesus emerged on the scene, though, the man approached and fell on his knees, saying, "What do you want with me, Jesus, Son of the Most High God? I beg you, don't torture me!" (v. 28).

There's a bit more dialogue in Mark's gospel—and it offers us some important details about possession worth pondering. Jesus asked the man for his name and the man said, "Legion," pointing to the notion that this particular man had more than one unclean spirit (v. 9). The details mirror much of what we're told in Matthew, with the demons begging not to be sent away and to be sent into the pigs.

Luke 8:31 also notes, though, that "they begged Jesus repeatedly not to order them to go into the Abyss." The most terrifying detail of the ordeal comes when Jesus granted that permission and we are told two thousand pigs in the herd subsequently drowned in the lake (Mark 5:13).

Mark and Luke give us some additional details before concluding by noting that the people, consumed by fear, asked Jesus to leave. The biblical writers mainly tell us of the shock some experienced when they reached the site of the incident and saw the formerly possessed man—a person who lived in tombs, acted animalistic, and was uncontrollably strong—suddenly docile and in his right mind.

Nowhere do the Scriptures show Christ pushing back against their pleas for them to leave, but as Jesus stepped on his boat to comply with their request, we glean some important details about the newly healed man from both Mark 5 and Luke 8. The Scriptures note that he begged to go with Christ, clearly showing yet another sign of spiritual change. Both Mark and Luke note that Christ told the man to instead go and tell his people how much God had done for him, and he complied, leaving many amazed by his story of restoration.

It's fascinating to explore all three chapters to glean essential details about the man (or men) in question and Jesus' handling of the healing. Why does one chapter say there are two men and the others describe a healing of a single individual? There are a variety of views and theories to consider, though GotQuestions.org perhaps offers the most plausible option:

Matthew tells us there were two demoniacs, while Mark and Luke only mention one of the two. It is unclear why they chose to mention only one, but that does not negate the possibility of a second demoniac being present. Mark and Luke do not say there was "only one" demon-possessed man. They simply state that one of the two met Jesus and spoke to Him. For whatever reason, Matthew simply gives us more information than Mark and Luke.[1]

The Christian resource goes on to note that a contradiction can only exist if one statement is made that makes another statement impossible or implausible.[2] This does not happen in this case, as it appears the only conundrum is that there is simply more information in one chapter than the others.

One final detail to mention that helps bolster this theory is the man's request that he go with Jesus. Perhaps only one of the men felt compelled to follow Jesus after the healing, and thus his story took precedence. This is merely a theory, but surely worthy of consideration.

JESUS, BEELZEBUL, AND RADICAL HEALING

Jesus' exorcisms and healings as described in Scripture were no doubt remarkable, but not everyone was on board with his tactics. Critics at the time denied that he was God's Son, with some questioning whether his power to expel demons was coming from a negative source. In fact, the Pharisees are seen in Matthew 12 pondering whether Jesus' power to expel demons came through "Beelzebul." The name might sound strange and unfamiliar, but the connotation and reality of their charge against Christ is disturbingly notable.

Matthew 12:24 gives a hint to the gravity of the claim when the Pharisees note that Beelzebul is "the prince of demons." Matthew also tells us that Jesus was brought "a demon-possessed man who was blind and mute" (12:22) and that Jesus healed him, allowing the man to both see and hear.

The people watching this were "astonished" and wondered if Jesus was "the Son of David" (v. 23). That's when the Pharisees attempted to drive the narrative in the opposite direction, proclaiming that Jesus could only expel demons through the power of Beelzebul.

Luke 11 also dives into this story, noting that the man Jesus healed was mute. This account adds in some additional details, including the skepticism expressed by some in the crowd. In addition to the Beelzebul claim, some wanted signs from heaven.

Rather than ignore the claim that he was somehow, through the power of a demon, driving out sinister forces, Jesus responded with a show-stopping proclamation:

> Jesus knew their thoughts and said to them: "Any kingdom divided against itself will be ruined, and a house divided against itself will fall. If Satan is divided against himself, how can his kingdom stand? I say this because you claim that I drive out demons by Beelzebul. Now if I drive out demons by Beelzebul, by whom do your followers drive them out? So then, they will be your judges. But if I drive out demons by the finger of God, then the kingdom of God has come upon you. (Luke 11:17–20)

And Christ wasn't done there; he delivered some statements about demons in verses 24–26 that warrant deeper exploration. Speaking of exorcism and expulsion of impure spirits, he said that a demon "goes through arid places seeking rest and does not find it" when that spirit is removed from a person (v. 24).

If this demon is able to reenter the person, the individual ends up in a worse place than he or she was before it was first expelled. This is something many experts have reported seeing in practice, which adds credence to these biblical accounts.

The Healing of a Possessed Little Boy

Each of the possession stories in the Bible hold important truths that can help us better understand the nature of evil, but there are two accounts in particular that cause many readers to pause in their tracks. The most terrifying and elusive elements of the account given in Matthew 17 and Mark 9 is the fact that the exorcism Jesus performs *involves a child*.

The common belief among many is that a person must personally do something that opens a spiritual door to the demonic, but these chapters seemingly call such definitive claims into question. We're not given much information about the how or why, but we are told Jesus exorcised the child after the boy's loving father approached, knelt before Christ, and asked him to help his little boy. The man said, "He has seizures and is suffering greatly. He often falls into the fire or into the water. I brought him to your disciples, but they could not heal him" (Matthew 17:15–16).

Mark 9:20 tells us that the demon immediately tossed the boy into convulsions at the sight of Jesus, once again showing Christ's authority over these spirits. The child dropped to the ground, rolled around, and foamed at the mouth. There's a truly remarkable—and human—dialogue that unfolds between the grieving father and Jesus, and it goes like this (Mark 9:21–24):

Jesus: "How long has he been like this?"

Boy's father: "From childhood. It has often thrown him into fire or water to kill him. But if you can do anything, take pity on us and help us."

Jesus: "'If you can'? Everything is possible for one who believes."

Boy's father: "I do believe; help me overcome my unbelief!"

Both Matthew and Mark tell us that Christ proceeded to help the boy, expelling the demon and immediately healing him. Mark 9:25 adds an intriguing detail that seems to differentiate this exorcism from others presented in the Scriptures. While Jesus made it clear that a demon could return to its host, he had a specific command for the spirit tormenting this boy: "Come out of him and never enter him again."

When the disciples later came to Jesus and asked why they couldn't remove the demon, Christ's response was convicting, especially in our material era—one that might lead many of us to ignore or downplay the spiritual realm. "Because you have so little faith," Jesus said. "Truly I tell you, if you have faith as small as a mustard seed, you can say to this mountain, 'Move from here to there,' and it will move. Nothing will be impossible for you" (Matthew 17:20).

THE FAITHFUL CANAANITE WOMAN

This boy's desperate father wasn't the only parent to plead with Jesus on behalf of his or her child. A Canaanite (Syrophoenician) woman successfully convinced Jesus to heal her daughter in a story that's presented in Matthew 15 and Mark 7.

The woman came to Jesus and cried out to him, revealing that her daughter was possessed by a demon and was "suffering terribly" (Matthew 15:22). Matthew doesn't tell us the girl's age, but Mark 7:25 describes her as the woman's "little daughter," causing us to believe that she, too, was a young child.

At first, Jesus was silent and his disciples told him to send the woman away, as she was crying aloud and most likely bothering them. But the Canaanite woman didn't give up. She knelt down before Jesus, called him "Lord," and continued to ask for his help. While he initially pushed back in what appeared to be a spiritual test, Jesus was moved by the woman's faith and granted her request.

"Woman, you have great faith!" Jesus said, instantaneously healing her daughter. "Your request is granted" (Matthew 15:28).

Interestingly, Matthew doesn't tell us whether the woman's afflicted daughter was with her during this conversation, but Mark 7:30 makes it clear that she was home at the time of the healing, showcasing the true power of Jesus' ability to exorcise demons. The verse tells us, "She went home and found her child lying on the bed, and the demon gone."

Again, it's hard to walk away from these two stories surrounding children and not ask "why?" Much of what we've discussed in this book focuses on people's free will—decisions made that experts believe invited the demonic into individuals' lives. But what do we make of children who find themselves afflicted? Have they, too, welcomed evil into their lives? And if so, are they accountable for such actions?

Norris, who admitted this is a theological area of struggle, noted that it's possible for people to find themselves dealing with issues from generations past. "I don't know why and I don't like it, but kids can deal with things from generations past," he said. "Why? I don't know . . . I can't tell you how many times I've seen someone delivered from an entry point of something they had nothing to do with."

He said the Bible speaks about generational curses and afflictions and that the profound brokenness that we see unfold in Genesis 3 has had lasting ramifications on humanity and our world at large. Paul told us that sin came into the world through Adam. "Sin entered the world through one man," he wrote, "and death through sin, and in this way death came to all people, because all sinned" (Romans 5:12).

It's clear that past sin sparked a domino effect on humanity, but it's hard to know for sure how this impacts children. Paul also told us about the power of Jesus' sacrifice for all of mankind:

> Consequently, just as one trespass resulted in condemnation for all people, so also one righteous act resulted in justification and life for all people. For just as through the disobedience of the one man the many were made sinners, so also through the obedience of the one man the many will be made righteous. (Romans 5:18–19)

So, through Christ, it seems true freedom is attainable. While Reverend Samuel Rodriguez said that the "multigenerational element" cannot be denied, he held firm that Jesus is the answer to severing any such issue. "The only thing that can break it is the blood of Jesus. If it's not embraced, there's a multigenerational element," he said. "We believe as Christians that we're not under generational curses; we're under generational blessings—that the moment we receive Jesus the curse is broken."

At the center of the discussion is the issue of parental rights and actions. What parents expose children to matters. If a parent is dabbling in the occult and placing their children around—or in—such activities, one would expect a potential fallout.

"If there is satanic oppression and possession and—not that you become enamored with it, but you embrace it or you tolerate it—that reality can actually transcend from one generation to another," Rodriguez said. "So, it's no surprise to me that there are children in Scripture that were possessed."

With this in mind, the preacher noted that any dabbling in darkness could potentially transfer over to others living in the same household. "Let's assume right now it's an entity, a demonic entity," Rodriguez said. "That entity that's in that household, do you think that entity is just going to stay with the adults?"

These proclamations are fascinating in light of stories like the

Ammons case out of Indiana. Pending the case is true and authentic, the mother was believed by experts to be the centerpiece of affliction, with the demonic issues jumping from her to the children.

At the least, these issues must be considered, as we're left with some curious scriptures on the matter. But since we are not told in the Bible about the cause of such afflictions, it's likely prudent to pull back from more definitively speculating.

THE HEALING OF THE MUTE MAN

Another one of the documented stories of exorcism in the New Testament is told in Matthew 9, when Jesus healed a man who was mute and could not talk. The man's circumstances were likely well known in his community, as his sudden ability to utter sound left people shocked.

There aren't many details mentioned about the conversation that unfolded before the exorcism, but Matthew 9 captures the utter amazement that Jesus' act spawned among onlookers. "And when the demon was driven out, the man who had been mute spoke," verse 33 reads. "The crowd was amazed and said, 'Nothing like this has ever been seen in Israel.'"

But the Pharisees said, "It is by the prince of demons that he drives out demons" (v. 34).

MARY MAGDALENE AND THE SEVEN DEMONS

Last but not least comes the exorcism of Mary Magdalene. We're not given much information on the process of what was said or done, but most Christians know Magdalene as one of Jesus' staunch and devoted followers. Her presence in Scripture is noteworthy, and it is clear that she decided to follow Christ after he healed her affliction.

Despite a lack of robust information on her exorcism experience, Luke 8 tells us that Mary Magdalene accompanied Jesus along with the twelve disciples. She was among "some women who had been cured of evil spirits and diseases" (Luke 8:2). It is here we learn that Jesus expelled seven demons from her—a proclamation repeated in Mark 16:9.

While this verse is among those (vv. 9–20) that do not appear in the earliest manuscripts, the fact is mentioned in Luke 8:2, which is not disputed. If anyone is looking for biblical evidence that shows the impact of the long-term healing someone can find in Christ, Mary's story is quite compelling.

She went on to follow Jesus to the end of his earthly life, witnessing most of his beatings and crucifixion—and the aftermath of the resurrection.[3] That's a pretty incredible legacy for a person who at one point is said to have suffered from the presence of seven demons.

There are so many incredible takeaways from the stories covered in this chapter—lessons about the importance and availability of heart change and life transformation through Christ. It's truly instructive to see how these spiritual maladies manifested and how hope and healing unfolded. Now that we've explored the powerful moments when Jesus overpowered evil, let's dive deeper into another complex conundrum: the purported causes of these afflictions.

PART THREE

OPENING THE DOOR

7

PATHWAYS TO SPIRITUAL QUICKSAND

There was a lot of feeling powerless. I did not enjoy the reality in which I lived, and so I sought after an escape."

Rob McKeown's experience mirrors the life struggles that millions of people face today. A product of divorce, he often felt powerless and rudderless as a child—circumstances that left him desperately searching for a way out.

"My escape started in my introduction to the occult and started through a game called Dungeons and Dragons," he said. "It always intrigued me, the thought that people could have this power that you experience through magic. I developed an interest in that."

As the years forged on and McKeown left childhood behind, he joined the military and became a young adult, but his interest in magic never subsided; his fascination with Dungeons and Dragons also persisted.

It all came to a climax one day, though, when he was playing the game with some fellow soldiers and one of his peers abruptly posed a fascinating question to the group: *"How would you like to experience the power and magic that you see here in real life?"*

After years of bottled-up intrigue, McKeown—whose interest was immediately piqued—answered affirmatively. And what happened next had a dire impact on his life.

"The guy bowed his head, and his eyes rolled back in his head, and a different French accented voice started speaking from him and talking to us," McKeown recalled. "He introduced himself as 'Valerian' and was telling us about this other realm where we had spirit guides that we could channel, and they could unlock our inner potential and spiritual abilities."

McKeown said he could immediately "feel the air change in the room a little bit." Then, he, too, got in on the action, and suddenly found himself "channeling" in a similar way.

At the time, he wasn't sure whether the experience was real, a game, or something in between, but he went along with it, feeding the unfulfilled intrigue he had kept inside since childhood.

As the experience unfolded, McKeown said the guy who initiated the channeling began spouting off details about McKeown's childhood—facts he couldn't have known. In that moment, McKeown knew something else was driving the dialogue.

"It wasn't his voice, and it said things about each one of us in the room that this guy would have no idea to know," he said. "It was very believable."

And that was the start of a strange and terrifying phase in McKeown's life. Suddenly, he, too, found himself "knowing things" he couldn't have possibly known. At first, he believed the spirits he had encountered were helping him on his path, as he started experiencing what he thought were helpful visions.

Meanwhile, people were randomly paying him old debts that were owed; his life circumstances seemed to be on a positive trajectory. But the situation soon changed.

His grandmother, who had a Pentecostal charismatic background, was aware of what was unfolding in McKeown's life, and she urged him to step away from the occult. In the end, her warnings were unsurprisingly prophetic, as McKeown's problems started to intensify.

He said he started to get turned off to the experience when he suddenly faced bouts of lost consciousness, finding himself dazed, confused, and in random places he didn't recall going. One night, McKeown's friends asked him to go to a club and he declined, noting that he needed to get ready for the next day and get some sleep.

"So, I did my stuff and I crashed," McKeown said, but he somehow ended up out and about without knowing it. "I woke up in the bar, fully dressed, drinking a beer, smoking a cigarette, and I did not take myself there."

This type of experience unfolded at least two or three times, as his spiritual battle intensified, with restraint and self-control slowly slipping away.

"I was struggling for control of me," McKeown said, adding that he also experienced torment and voices. "I thought I was in control of these things, and now these things seemed to be taking more and more control of me. Fear was setting in."

As this internal clash unfolded, the voices became more pronounced and chaotic.

"I remember arguments that were going on in my head where it was all like, 'No, I get to use him tonight. I'm going to take control,'" McKeown said.

His grandmother was still fervently praying for him and routinely sending him Bible verses; she also explained her belief that these "spirit guides" he thought were helping him were actually demonic forces bent on harming him.

McKeown listened to her but wasn't yet convinced. It wasn't until a more dramatic moment during a nightclub fight totally changed his mind. Amid the scuffle, McKeown said it was as though he was "present" but was "thrown to the back" of his own mind and was "watching through binoculars, backwards."

"I had a very small vision, a glimpse of what was going on. I could hear it, I could mostly see it, but my arm, my right hand shot out and grabbed him around his throat and kind of lifted him up off of the ground and then threw him to the ground, and I put my knee in his chest," he said, noting that it was as though the voices wanted him to kill the man.

McKeown felt himself pushing back against the inclination to harm his opponent, and before he knew it he was back in control of his body; he stepped off the guy and was trembling.

"The voices started going bananas in my head," he said. "It was like, 'You're weak, you're worthless. If you can't kill him, we demand blood. We want you to kill yourself.'"

McKeown said the nightclub experience was his breaking point. He went back to his barracks that night and started furiously pacing around, thinking over all he had experienced.

His roommate was so shaken by his behavior that he threatened to take him to a psychiatrist if he didn't piece himself together.

It was in that moment that McKeown started the process of making a commitment that would forever transform his life.

"I hit my knees and I said, 'God, if you're there, help me because I don't know what I'm doing," he said. "The voices immediately went quiet."

McKeown didn't officially accept Christ that night. In fact, it wasn't until he was channel surfing one day and stumbled upon Trinity Broadcast Network, where he heard a preacher present the gospel, and he finally made the decision to become a Christian. The message on the screen perfectly fit McKeown's story—and compelled him to action.

"The preacher said, 'I'm just feeling led by the Holy Spirit to lead this prayer again. There's somebody out there, you've been involved in occultic activity,'" McKeown recalled. "He basically just read my mind, adding, 'You grew up in a home around Christianity and you've always rejected it and you're in trouble and God wants you to know this is for you.'"

McKeown continued, "I dropped my beer, and I asked Jesus into my heart."

He never again heard those voices, and went on to attend a charismatic Bible college, building his faith along the way. While it was initially a struggle to keep his faith in line, McKeown said he persisted and is blessed to have the life God has given him.

"Being able to conduct my own thoughts and being able to enjoy the things in life that God has provided for me have been a bigger joy than what I thought," he said, adding a message for others who might be struggling with spiritual warfare. "God loves you completely and thoroughly, and he has provided some really great things for you to experience in your life if you will let him. He's the only one that can provide freedom."

Let's explore the main takeaway. Pop culture's lens into the alarming impact of demons, possession, and infestation is well represented in movies and television, with the effects of spiritual warfare often playing out in characters' lives in over-the-top form. But there's often a dearth of focus on understanding the pathways that can lead a person to burst through diabolical doorways and into the center of spiritual quicksand.

Many times, the effect of the affliction is often spotlighted, while the cause is typically treated like an afterthought. Admittedly, the Bible, which recounts numerous possession stories, doesn't give us a great deal of information surrounding the "how."

In the Old Testament we do see Saul disobeying God before an evil spirit is sent to torment him.[1] "Now the Spirit of the LORD had departed from Saul, and an evil spirit from the LORD tormented him," 1 Samuel 16:14 reads, with verses 15 and 16 continuing, "Saul's attendants said to him, 'See, an evil spirit from God is tormenting you. Let our lord command his servants here to search for someone who can play the lyre. He will play when the evil spirit from God comes on you, and you will feel better.'"

David was chosen to play this instrument, with verse 23 explaining that "whenever the spirit from God came on Saul, David would take up his lyre and play." Interestingly, relief would then follow and "the evil spirit would leave him." There's much more to unpack there, but we can surmise that this spirit was the result of Saul's disobedience[2] and that God offered healing with an opening for repentance—one Saul never took.[3] But other stories in the Bible surrounding possession and evil aren't as detailed.

With that in mind, anyone who believes in the demonic realm is faced with an essential question: What, if anything, can open a person up to being oppressed or possessed? Answering this question is the primary objective of this chapter—one that many faith leaders and theologians seemed anxious to clarify.

"All of the spiritual realm, whether we're talking holy or unholy, is permission based. All of it," Dr. Shane Wood replied when I posed this very question. "No one falls into salvation any more than someone accidentally gets possessed. It's permission that is granted."

This is akin to a door or hallway that a person willingly walks through, taking concerted steps along the way. As human beings approach these spiritual doors, turn the knobs, and intentionally stroll through, many times they have no idea what they'll encounter on the other side, yet curiosity still propels some to strut into the unknown.

Once the permission side of the equation is understood, it's essential to define the difference between *oppression* and *possession*, the two terms typically used to differentiate between various degrees of demonic affliction.

Matt Slick of the Christian Apologetics and Research Ministry defined demonic oppression as "the work of evil spiritual forces that urge us to sin, to deny God's Word, to feel spiritually dead, and to be in bondage to sinful things."[4] Slick added in an explainer on the issue that these forces work against Christians and non-Christians alike, and that their central goal is to "bring as many people as possible into rebellion against God and condemnation in hell."[5]

There is surely debate about how oppression manifests, though Slick argues it can come through anxiety, sleeplessness, anger toward God, fascination with various religious systems, emotional issues, and financial crises, among other conundrums.[6] He warned, though, that these issues might actually have nothing at all to do with spiritual matters and could instead be the result of our own poor decision making; he encouraged prayer to help overcome anything that appears to be rooted in true oppression.

> *As human beings approach these spiritual doors, turn the knobs, and intentionally stroll through, many times they have no idea what they'll encounter on the other side, yet curiosity still propels some to strut into the unknown.*

With all that in mind, how does oppression differ from possession? While oppression is more of a spiritual pressure put upon human beings, possession is an all-encompassing experience. *Possess* is defined by *Merriam-Webster* as "to enter into and control firmly," and this is exactly how the Bible expresses the act of demonic possession. In the case of demonic possession, evil forces overtake a person's body, eliciting total control at moments of speech, movement, and action.

This is what we can explore throughout the New Testament Scriptures and in stories about the Ammons family, Robbie, and many others. As we've observed thus far, many experts believe that possession is rare and is generally reserved for nonbelievers, while oppression is seen as something that targets Christians and non-Christians alike.

How Demonic Oppression Manifests

Now that those clarifications are out of the way, let's get back to the causal question: What opens people up to these demonic forces? Let's start with the biblical texts. The Scriptures fervently implore humans to base our lives on God and his standards. James 4:7 specifically offers Christians a simple yet powerful reminder to follow God and reject evil: "Submit yourselves, then, to God. Resist the devil, and he will flee from you." While this hardly gives us the full picture of the demonic realm, it clearly calls us to live for God and to shun and reject anything outside of his realm.

Based on Scripture, we can assume that demonic oppression or infestation can elevate or permeate people's lives, especially when people flagrantly reject the call to resist evil and cling to God's standards. Pastor Lucas Miles described this spiritual dynamic of oppression as unfolding when "there tends to be an agreement with something other than the truth of the Word or Christ himself." This is a general definition that lends itself to some sweeping possibilities.

Spiritual oppression might come in benign forms for many, with a specific act or mindset yielding problematic behavior that offers evil a place of power or influence over one's life. Some theologians and pastors argue that it can be rooted in a simple yet unfortunate step of allowing hatred or anger to rule over one's life, giving these emotions permission to both manifest and grow.

Unrepentant and perpetual sin is another one of the catalysts that some pinpoint, believing that the refusal to stop sinning can, over time, open a person up to demonic attack. Perhaps the most common of these purported causes, though, is the slippery and un-intended moral slope. It is often in unanticipated and slow-moving circumstances that we find expansive and gaping holes that allow in life-altering evil.

Dr. Michael Brown offered a hypothetical illustration about the pitfalls and dangers of spiritual slopes, describing a man who is frustrated in his marriage and finds himself unguarded:

> So, here's a married man and he's unhappy. He and his wife are fighting a lot. They're under financial pressure. But there's this young gal at work and she thinks his jokes are so funny, and they start to get a little more friendly. And the next thing, they're texting a little bit, and before he knows it, he's gripped. It's not just an emotional thing. There's a spiritual bond that's taken place and now he's trying to get free and doesn't know how.

Brown emphasized the true danger that manifests from opening the wrong doors in life—routes that can lead us toward truly damaging destinations. "We open up doors, we go in the wrong direction, and then we get into dangerous territory," he said. "And the progression you'll see is that the sin that once satisfied, even temporarily, doesn't satisfy at all. It leads to more sins, worse sins, and then it enslaves. And at that point, we can be bound by the devil himself."

In addition to being spiritually unguarded, some of us choose anger and pride—emotions that can destroy our spiritual standing. Miles shared the real-life example of a man who claimed to face demonic episodes after experiencing intense difficulties as a child.

His mother was abused by his father, and after asking God to step in to stop the abuse and not receiving immediate reprieve, the child looked elsewhere for power. "He had this encounter that he talks about where he felt like he made an agreement with the devil. . . . 'If you give me the strength to overcome this, I'll follow you,'" Miles recounted.

One day, the kid grabbed a baseball bat while his dad was hurting his mother and chased his father out of the house; it was a defining moment in his life—but for all the wrong reasons. "He made an agreement with his anger . . . he could rely on his anger more so than he could rely on the Lord to deliver him from situations," Miles said. "So, whenever he came against problems in his life, he reached back to that agreement, and he reached back to utilizing anger as a way to overcome, rather than peace, love, kindness, etcetera."

One can see how this damages a person over time, opening up the door to potential oppression. Our decisions, relationships, and the overarching trajectories of our lives can directly impact our spiritual condition.

"It's the question of, what doors am I opening in my own life?" Brown said, going on to point out pornography use to illustrate his position. "We understand that pornography is addictive like a drug is addictive, just on a physiological level—that someone who is heavily addicted to porn and spending hours and hours a day with porn, that their brain is getting wired differently."

But rather than merely physical or mental, an issue like this, Brown argued, is also spiritual, and can have dire implications for the person engaging in it. "As it is in the natural, so it is in the spiritual," he said, "that you begin to open yourself up to certain things." This is why theologians and pastors will warn Christians to follow close to their faith, appealing to God and seeking out his standards.

There are also traumatic or tragic life events that can leave us off-kilter and, if we're not careful, lead us on a downward spiritual spiral.

"Traumatic events in our life, whether it's drug use, whether it's distorted experiences of sexuality, physical harm—all these things—those emotional and physical events are more conducive for us to make agreements with . . . what I would call demonic emotions or demonic lies or demonic viewpoints," Miles added.

For his part, Reverend Benjamin McEntire said mental and spiritual afflictions often originate from trauma and negative experiences from a person's past, and that trauma can many times be "an open door for the enemy."

And one mental health expert who wished to remain anonymous

agreed, noting that most of his patients have faced past sexual abuse that has made their lives "become hell." From emotions to horrific experiences and unresolved trauma, the conditions that impact the human spirit are plentiful—and we're only scratching the surface here.

Miles also pointed to fame as a potential doorway into spiritual problems, providing an example of a famous pastor, who might find himself on stage and relishing in success, beginning to believe that he ascended to that position by his or her own merits and not by God's provision.

It's these sorts of "lies" that can become spiritually problematic, with Miles adding that none of us are immune to such mistruths. "Every single belief that we have and choice that we have, it's always an opportunity to either believe what God said or to believe what the enemy says," he said. "And that same choice that comes back to the garden—'Are we going to believe the serpent, or are we going to believe the King?'"

Experts on this topic often focus on the potential spiritual cracks that can allow evil to seep into human's lives—a focus that I find quite interesting. People tend to focus more on dramatic possession events that garner a plethora of attention, but the most subtle issues are said to be more plentiful and pervasive. And in a world in which so many diminish or ignore the spiritual realm, our culture is desperately in need of these reminders.

"You never want to go in the wrong direction with your life, especially with the spiritual realm," Brown said. "It is very real. It is very dangerous."

Looking for Power in All the Wrong Places

Curiosity is part of the human experience that can drive people toward marvelous and life-changing discoveries. Our ability to wonder and search for answers is what catapults so many visionaries to achieve transformational success. But our inquisitive nature can also lead us to seek answers in some of the worst possible places—frontiers we were never meant to explore. When we fail to fill our natural spiritual voids with truth, we risk inundating our hearts with lies.

Dr. Michael Heiser, a well-known Bible scholar, pointedly addressed this phenomenon, explaining that mismanaging our voids and our natural curiosities can yield negative assumptions, improper actions, and a seductive scenario that leads to spiritual blights. From consulting psychics to attempts to use the Ouija board, the potential entry points of evil are practically limitless.

> *When we fail to fill our natural spiritual voids with truth, we risk inundating our hearts with lies.*

These tools, though not always taken seriously, are relied on as points of contact and communication with the unseen realm—one we know very little about. Many assume they are in full control of how these interactions will unfold, but experts warn that this mindset couldn't be further from the truth.

"There's a seduction, either that is learned through pop culture or reading . . . or experimentation, where people are led to believe that they can control the circumstances of the engagement, whatever that is," Heiser said. "That they're in control, that they will be able to tell where the lines are and when they've crossed them, or shouldn't cross them."

Heiser contends that there's often a mixture of deceptive elements and an overestimation of our own abilities when it comes to the spiritual realm. He posed an essential question to anyone who has considered diving into these antics: "If this is foreign to our experience, if this is a reality that we are not by nature part of, how could we possibly expect to be able to understand it and control it?"

Heiser said many fail to pause and adequately consider this

question, and when you mix that failure with the cartoonish and lighthearted lens through which culture generally treats tools like the Ouija board, it's no surprise why so many people jump right into the deep end.

"When they get 'results' out of it, there's a seductive element to it," he added. "Like, 'Wow, I've tapped into secret knowledge now. I know things that other people don't. I know things that my pastor doesn't, or those church people don't. Boy, I've got a leg up on them.'" This amalgam of arrogance, pride, invigoration, and fascination only adds to the toxic seduction—a combustible combination that can absolutely swallow us up and spit us out.

While working as a faith and culture reporter, I encountered numerous claims of this sort over the years. And throughout my many years working in New York City I've often stumbled upon street signs advertising psychic services. These random placards usually catch my eye as I'm strolling through Manhattan on my way to a meeting or interview.

The ads, which entice passersby with promises to deliver intuitive reflections and prophecies, are almost always next to narrow staircases that lead to elusive upper floors—locations where people go to seek hope, messages from beyond the grave, and predictions about their futures. Others simply seek psychics for the mere fun of it.

Biblically speaking, there's no case to be made for a Christian engaging in such activities, with Scripture recommending total avoidance—and repentance—for those who do. For many, the idea of a psychic seems ridiculous and impractical, a grand scheme to sucker people out of their money, and that's understandable. Surely, some—or even many—of those who purport to have these powers are swindling and tricking the masses, though a solid look at Scripture delivers some important realities and warnings worth considering.

The Bible seems to affirm that these individuals exist, as the text openly implores people not to practice or seek out psychics' services.

As we'll explore, it's a reality that flows throughout both the New and Old Testaments.

What the Bible Says About Psychics and Mediums

The Old Testament doesn't shy away from these topics, with Leviticus 19:26 reading, "Do not practice divination or seek omens." And Leviticus 19:31 adds, "Do not turn to mediums or seek out spiritists, for you will be defiled by them. I am the Lord your God."

These verses, along with other content in Leviticus, were written by Moses specifically for the Israelites, but there seem to be some interesting and timeless elements worth noting. Not only do these verses indicate that there were people who practiced divination (seeking supernatural information about the future), but the Israelites were also urged to steer clear of anyone who sought out communication with the dead.

And that's hardly the only place where this issue emerges in Scripture. These same themes appear in Deuteronomy 18:9–13, with heavier-handed wording and warnings:

> When you enter the land the Lord your God is giving you, do not learn to imitate the detestable ways of the nations there. Let no one be found among you who sacrifices their son or daughter in the fire, who practices divination or sorcery, interprets omens, engages in witchcraft, or casts spells, or who is a medium or spiritist or who consults the dead. Anyone who does these things is detestable to the Lord; because of these same detestable practices the Lord your God will drive out those nations before you. You must be blameless before the Lord your God.

When one continues to read through Scripture, these elements emerge again and again, with Isaiah questioning why a person would consult "mediums and spiritualists." He proclaimed:

> When someone tells you to consult mediums and spiritists, who whisper and mutter, should not a people inquire of their God? Why consult the dead on behalf of the living? Consult God's instruction and the testimony of warning. If anyone does not speak according to this word, they have no light of dawn. (Isaiah 8:19–20)

Leviticus 20:27 goes even further, condemning the practice entirely. The jarring verse reads: "A man or woman who is a medium or spiritist among you must be put to death. You are to stone them; their blood will be on their own heads." This harsh penalty under Old Testament law makes one reality immensely clear: reliance on mediums and spiritualists was not only condemned but was also seen as a major violation of trust in God and morality more generally.

People have continued to debate these verses, including the severe penalty in Leviticus 20:27, but a clear reading of these Scriptures leaves the reader with no other option but to, at the least, understand the perceived severity of this spiritual breach. We find an example of this dynamic playing out in 1 Chronicles 10:13–14, which tells us that King Saul died because of his unfaithfulness to God. In addition to failing to keep his word to the Lord, these verses reveal that he "even consulted a medium for guidance" before his demise.

This story is recounted in earlier writings in 1 Samuel 28, where we learn more details about Saul consulting the medium. The Scriptures explain that Samuel has died and that Saul had "expelled the mediums and spiritists from the land" (v. 3). But we quickly see that Saul was filled with immense terror when the Philistines assembled against him. So, after going to God for help and not receiving any answers, Saul decided to take matters into his own hands, asking those around him to locate a medium.

Saul proceeded to disguise himself and go out to meet the woman, giving her a shocking command: "Consult a spirit for me, . . . and bring up for me the one I name" (v. 8). The woman was initially hesitant, as she didn't realize she was communicating with Saul—the man who had expelled mediums from the land. But she noted the king's condemnation of mediums, yet inevitably relented and granted Saul's request: that she conjure Samuel. This is where the story takes a bit of a dramatic turn, with the medium finding herself shocked to see Samuel emerge from beyond the grave.

Saul proceeded to speak with Samuel, seeking his guidance and help. "I am in great distress. . . . The Philistines are fighting against me, and God has departed from me," Saul told Samuel. "He no longer answers me, either by prophets or by dreams. So I have called on you to tell me what to do" (v. 15).

Saul's admission showed a true lack of faith, and Samuel's reaction did little to bring him any solace. Samuel noted that God had become Saul's enemy, and that Saul was being punished for not listening to the Lord. He added, "The LORD will deliver both Israel and you into the hands of the Philistines, and tomorrow you and your sons will be with me. The LORD will also give the army of Israel into the hands of the Philistines" (v. 19).

Saul's death is recorded in 1 Samuel 31. The story sparks many theological questions, and we cannot get into all of them. But the biblical warnings and realities surrounding mediums should at a minimum cause us some pause, specifically if we are practicing Christians. These biblical mentions don't end with Saul though. In 2 Kings 21, we meet King Manasseh of Judah and we are told that he "did evil in the eyes of the LORD" (v. 2) and followed the traditions of foreign cultures, building altars to foreign gods. All of this, the Bible tells us, sparked God's anger.

But the most horrific piece of his story is told in 2 Kings 21:6, which reads, "He sacrificed his own son in the fire, practiced divination, sought omens, and consulted mediums and spiritists. He did much evil in the eyes of the LORD, arousing his anger." Once again, we see mediums and divination being presented in a negative light.

When we move to the New Testament, we see some activities unfolding in Acts 16 that seem to further address these issues. It is in this chapter that we meet a female slave who is described as having "a spirit by which she predicted the future" (v. 16). This language is fascinating and opens up questions about what, exactly, caused her supernatural ability to predict various happenings. We are told that this woman clearly had this ability, and that she earned a lot of money for her owners by engaging in fortune-telling.

One day, she confronted Paul and simply wouldn't leave him and his followers alone. "She followed Paul and the rest of us, shouting, 'These men are servants of the Most High God, who are telling you the way to be saved.' She kept this up for many days," Luke wrote (vv. 17–18).

Paul started to become irritated by the woman's presence, though. So, as Luke wrote, Paul "turned around and said to the spirit, 'In the name of Jesus Christ I command you to come out of her!'" It's fascinating to note that Paul addressed the spirit inside the woman, and that he commanded this spirit to leave her at once, to which it complied.

The slave woman was clearly delivered, but her owners were angry at Paul and Silas after they realized they would no longer be able to profit off of her abilities. Paul and Silas were dragged off, beaten, and jailed, but the decision to expel the spirit inside of the woman leaves us with further clues that her fortune-telling abilities were not a positive attribute, and were, in fact, one from which she needed deliverance.

If we backtrack again to the Old Testament, there are some

additional verses worth mentioning in this discussion. Heiser pointed to Deuteronomy 13:1–5 as a set of verses that are sometimes overlooked—scriptures that read:

> If a prophet, or one who foretells by dreams, appears among you and announces to you a sign or wonder, and if the sign or wonder spoken of takes place, and the prophet says, "Let us follow other gods" (gods you have not known) "and let us worship them," you must not listen to the words of that prophet or dreamer. The LORD your God is testing you to find out whether you love him with all your heart and with all your soul. It is the LORD your God you must follow, and him you must revere. Keep his commands and obey him; serve him and hold fast to him. That prophet or dreamer must be put to death for inciting rebellion against the LORD your God, who brought you out of Egypt and redeemed you from the land of slavery. That prophet or dreamer tried to turn you from the way the LORD your God commanded you to follow. You must purge the evil from among you.

Heiser unpacked these verses and emphasized what he sees as the clarity of their meaning: that the Bible notes these "psychic" abilities are possible but can lead to misleading conclusions. "You have an instance where you have a person claiming to be the prophet . . . who can predict something that comes to pass, or can do a sign and wonder, and the passage is very clear," he said. "If that person and this experience, or this thing they do, leads you in such a way that is contrary to what the Lord has taught you, that person is condemned."

Heiser continued, "So what it tells us is that people can actually do these things, and they'll look like what you think is from God, but it's not." But how does a person end up with these abilities? The Bible speaks a great deal about prophets; a prophet is a person "who utters divinely inspired revelations" from God.[7] But that's not what Heiser is speaking about here.

According to the Bible, a prophet gets reliable revelation directly from the Lord—and that information never violates biblical truth. Others who mirror these abilities on the psychic side would not, in the mind of Heiser and others, be getting their abilities from the Almighty. Heiser believes the people who have these capabilities are getting them from a source outside of God and that there can typically be some family history or other entry point that has enabled these experiences and perspectives to take hold.

"There's some entry points, there's some attachment somewhere within their family, or their sphere of contacts, that leads to them having experiences," he said. "And then, of course, they're encouraged to parse them one way . . . and then away they go."

A broader conversation is certainly warranted surrounding the root cause of these abilities, but the more essential point is that, regardless of these scriptures and warnings, many still engage in and seek out these spiritual activities thousands of years after biblical warnings were delivered to the Israelites as well as those living in the New Testament era.

Much of this behavior has been normalized in pop culture, too, even as theologians and experts who work in the spiritual warfare realm openly warn that engaging in these practices can be dangerous, serving as negative pathways into a person's soul. So, the message at the start of this chapter once again becomes paramount: stand firm with the Lord and abide by his standards.

Reverend Samuel Rodriguez is among those who believe Satan's plan is to "either possess or attempt to oppress"—a strategy that has infiltrated people's lives and helped separate individuals from God's love.

"If you don't have a firewall of righteousness, if you're not covered by the vicarious atoning work of Jesus, then possession is really a possibility, especially those that dabble with darkness and dabble into satanic witchcraft, convocations, calling upon spirits and so forth, engage in activity that is really outside the norms of what we would call appropriate," he told me, "literally provoking darkness to invade their lives."

There are, of course, many ways to "provoke darkness." Some pervasive and all-encompassing activities like Satanic worship are clearly problematic, though experts believe that other activities like Ouija board–use can also have a dire impact.

Drug Abuse and the Spiritual Realm

This idea of "provoking darkness" is an intriguing one, as it causes one to wonder what other activities could potentially open up a person to spiritual oppression. Interestingly, drug use was mentioned by a number of interview subjects as yet another potential doorway to the demonic, with Miles, among others, noting his belief that there is a potential connection between using illicit substances and opening a pathway into evil.

"There's something about this breaking of the brain-blood barrier in specifically illicit drugs," he said. "It's opening up a door to a realm of this sort of distorted mental and emotional capacity that was really never intended to be open."

Slick noted in his own writings that the Bible "does not talk about drugs in the sense of our modern understanding with antibiotics, pain killers, and hallucinogenics," and, as a result, "we cannot definitively say that drugs cause demonic possession."[8]

But, to Miles's point, he noted what can happen when a person is "enslaved" to drugs or substances is an altered state as a result of usage.[9] In this case, Slick wrote that drugs can "affect a person sufficiently to contribute to demonic oppression and/or possession."

One expert who asked not to be named said that people might get into drugs innocently but that the spiritual ramifications are quite stark. "There's a demon with every drug, particularly when you're coming through dealers . . . they're definitely attached," he said. "There's not a person who's addicted . . . there's a demon spirit that's causing that."

Brown detailed his own descent into drugs, noting that he started getting high on marijuana when he was fourteen years old—and soon found himself diving deeper than he could have ever imagined into much more serious and dangerous substances. "You get used to a particular thing. Now, it creates a hunger and an appetite for more," Brown explained. "What used to scintillate doesn't scintillate anymore . . . so you need to do something a little harder, a little stronger, and then your conscience gets hardened in the process and then you start hanging out with people you wouldn't have hung out with before."

He said that this dynamic can play out and lead to some damaging arenas, with people suddenly finding themselves acting in ways they would have never imagined. This was the case in Brown's own journey into the drug abyss.

"I went from smoking pot at fourteen to shooting heroin at fifteen," he said. "That's a picture of what happens in the spiritual realm or the demonic realm, that you begin to open yourself up. You begin to entertain certain things; you begin to step in a wrong direction and Satan is going to seize that."

Brown's story is unique in that he "got radically saved" at age sixteen—just two years after he started down a negative path, reversing course and springing toward God and away from drugs and substances. Plenty of people find healing from drug and substance abuse, and regardless of where people stand on the spiritual connection, avoiding these elements is clearly prudent.

PLAYING WITH FIRE YIELDS DARKNESS

Spiritually speaking, most theologians and pastors agree that there are many ways in which "playing with fire" can usher in spiritual darkness. While most agree that full-on demonic possession is a rare phenomenon, it seems the deeper, more prevalent issue is oppression, which can arrive and manifest in a plethora of ways.

"There are those who are oppressed by darkness, and then there are those who have to fight off darkness because darkness is emerging to distract," Rodriguez explained. "Darkness may not penetrate, it may not invade, but will attempt to distract."

> *There are many ways in which "playing with fire" can usher in spiritual darkness.*

Distraction can sometimes be the first step toward something more prevalent or pervasive. So the goal is to avoid falling into these slippery slopes and spiritual traps. Pastors and theologians interviewed for this book pointed to the importance of a healthy spiritual life filled with prayer, Scripture reading, reflection, and a tight-knit relationship with God.

The spiritual blueprint is before us; what remains is a simple question for every human being: Will we follow it?

8

THE OUIJA BOARD

The Ouija board almost always emerges amid discussions about the pitfalls of playing with fire. Some dismiss the game as simple and harmless, while others see it as a diabolical window into the spirit world—a tool that can open users up to demonic influence, spiritual suffering, and truly detrimental experiences.

On one hand, millions play the game, with the vast majority experiencing little more than playful giggles and mild jitters. But on the other, some have claimed the Ouija experience has torn open for them a personal portal to spiritual pandemonium.

There are countless stories of people claiming unexplainable phenomena after playing the game. These claims, which are understandably met with skepticism, seem to challenge or at least call into question the common framing of the board as a mere parlor game.

A brief exploration of Amazon reviews of

> *Some have claimed the Ouija experience has torn open for them a personal portal to spiritual pandemonium.*

the Ouija board offers up a litany of proclamations that the board is a fake and a fraud, though not everyone is so sure.

"This thing has ruined my life," one purchaser wrote. "It has made my home a horrible place lights will turn off out of nowhere and I followed all of the rules and it is put to harm me and my family."[1] Another person added, "Now I have to move away. Use at your own risk."[2]

There are other reviews making similar claims. There is no way to know if these assertions are simply mock attempts to scare purchasers (the reviewers in these two cases notably gave the product one star) or something more sinister.

There is something else quite fascinating amid the mix of reviews though: comments from people who aren't verified purchasers but who intentionally posted on Amazon in an effort to dissuade people from buying the board.

"I can't talk about the quality of this object, but I can talk about the experience. I cannot advise more strongly against any attempt to use this board," one reviewer wrote. "Trust me, I know what will happen, I have experienced it. Please please take my advice, do not buy this. I can't guarantee whether you will come out of this as well as we did. Please please take my advice, do not buy this."[3]

So, what's the real deal with the Ouija board? Is it truly a portal to spirits—or a benign and harmless distraction with no more spiritual power than any other table game? Dr. Michael Brown is among those who warn people to be wary of the Ouija board, explaining that some who dabble in the occult believe the board is "one of the standard entry points" to the spirit world.

"You're trying to get in tune with supernatural knowledge, with supernatural information; you're trying to make contact with another realm," he said. "And even if for a lot of people nothing really happens and it's just a piece of wood or whatever, the goal is to make something happen."

Make no mistake: the entire draw of the Ouija board is that it openly professes to knock down a spiritual barrier. Sold by toy giant Hasbro, the Ouija board's official sales language promises to let users into the "world of the mysterious and mystifying," offering people ages eight and up answers from "the spirit world."[4]

"Ask your question with a friend using the planchette that comes with the board, but be patient and concentrate because the spirits can't be rushed," the description continues. "Handle the Ouija board with respect and it won't disappoint you!"

This description hasn't changed all that much since 1891, when the toy was advertised in the *Pittsburgh Dispatch*. An ad at the time said that the board's "mysterious movements invite the most careful research and investigation—apparently forming the link which unites the known with the unknown, the material with the immaterial."[5]

Many people laugh off the increased popularity of the Ouija board, opting to use it for laughs and entertainment. Meanwhile, pastors, priests, and faith leaders like Brown have repeatedly and increasingly sounded the alarm that its use can lead to a dire spiritual scenario.

These warnings have only intensified in recent years alongside skyrocketing sales of the Ouija board. Purchases were said to have grown 300 percent in 2014 after the release of Hollywood horror film *Ouija*, a movie based on the popular game board; a follow-up film titled *Ouija: Origin of Evil* was released in 2016.[6] One outlet called the spike in sales an "unexpected renaissance," with increased attention in Hollywood and culture apparently catapulting people's interest.[7]

Warnings about the Ouija board aren't tucked away or hidden in the quiet corners of the theological realm, either, as some faith leaders have openly turned to prominent media outlets to warn about the purported dangers of using the board. Peter Irwin-Clark, a Church of England vicar, told the *Daily Mail* in a 2014 interview that parents simply shouldn't allow their children to use the tool. "It's like opening a shutter in one's soul and letting in the supernatural," Irwin-Clark said.[8] "There are spiritual realities out there and they can be very negative. It is absolutely appalling. I would very strongly advise parents not to buy Ouija boards for children."

Before we go deeper into spiritual claims about the board, it's perhaps necessary to dive into its origins, which are strange and mysterious to say the least. One of the most remarkable facts about the Ouija board is that its general design and appearance hasn't radically changed much over the years. It has essentially always been a board with letters of the alphabet, numbers zero through nine, and the words *yes, no,* and *goodbye.*[9]

And there has apparently always been a planchette—the device that is said to move around the board, exposing letters and numbers in ordered fashion. But while there is a multitude of information about the board's impact on users, the details behind its origins have always been a bit clouded in uncertainty and fantastical claims. It wasn't until 1992 when a man named Robert Murch started digging deeper into the Ouija board and its history that some clearer claims and details started to come to fruition.

The roots of the board were set in the mid-nineteenth century when America experienced what *Smithsonian* magazine called an "obsession with spiritualism" and the belief that the living could communicate with the dead.[10] By 1886, the Associated Press was reporting on the new emergence of so-called talking boards, and by 1890 a group of businessmen led by Charles Kennard, from Baltimore, had come together to figure out a way to monetize the new tool.[11]

At that point, Kennard and his team—which included attorney Elijah Bond and Col. Washington Bowie—formed the Kennard Novelty Company, but they hadn't yet come up with a name for the talking board. Murch told *Smithsonian* magazine that it was Bond's sister-in-law, Helen Peters, a purported medium, who is said to have conjured up the name after *asking the board* what they should call it.[12]

A US patent granted for the Ouija board on February 10, 1891, includes images of the board and lists Bond as the inventor.[13] The patent describes the toy in detail and proclaims that the men sought "to produce a toy or game by which two or more persons can amuse themselves by asking questions of any kind and having them answered by the device used and operated by the touch of the hand."

Not much is known about what unfolded at the US Patent Office, though the creators used the fact that the Ouija board was granted a patent in advertising language to help sell the product, with one newspaper ad in the late 1800s proclaiming that "Ouija was thoroughly tested at the United States Patent Office before the patent was allowed."[14]

Murch told *Time* one of the backstories that has circulated about how the board was given a patent; getting a successful patent purportedly involved proving that the board worked as advertised:

So Elijah Bond files for the patent, and the patent office says, you have to prove it works. A grandson of Helen Peters says his grandmother told his family this story: Bond took Peters to the patent office in Washington, D.C. They show it to the first clerk, who says, "I don't want to be a laughing stock." They get the chief clerk, who says, "If that contraption can spell out my name, then you've got your patent." Peters takes out the Ouija Board. It spells his name. The chief clerk—visibly shaken—says, "O.K. you've got your patent." But the patent doesn't talk about why it works.[15]

The patent process aside, one fact is undeniable: it didn't take long for these so-called talking boards to become a big hit, with San Francisco's the *Morning Call* reporting in 1893 that "planchette fever" had broken out in Northern California, noting that people were "anxious to hold communion with the dead and distant living."[16]

The Kennard Novelty Company eventually expanded to a second factory in Baltimore and opened locations in New York, Chicago, and London. Within a few years, *Smithsonian* noted that Bond and Kennard were no longer involved with the company, and that it was being run by a man named William Fuld.[17]

Now, Fuld's story is one of the strangest elements in the history of the Ouija board's evolution. His life came to a tragic end on February 26, 1927, with the *New York Times* publishing a February 27 obituary titled, "Ouija Board Inventor Dies in Fall Off Roof: Fuld Loses His Balance While Placing New Flag Pole on His Toy Factory."[18]

According to the obituary, Fuld fell "three stories to the street from the roof of his toy factory." Here's more:

> Mr. Fuld had gone to the roof to superintend the replacement of a worn-out flagpole. He was standing near the edge of the roof, balancing himself by grasping an iron support of the pole, according to the workmen, when the support pulled from its moorings and Mr. Fuld toppled over backward and fell to the ground.[19]

The *Times* article, which seems to incorrectly label Fuld as the creator of the board, doesn't mention some of the other purported details of the story—mainly that Fuld claimed the board told him to build the very factory from which he fell and died.[20] It's a strange story indeed, but one worthy of recounting in light of the board's ongoing infamy.

The popularity of the Ouija board has ebbed and flowed over the years, with times of uncertainty such as war purportedly driving more interest and usage. Spiritualism itself exploded during the Civil War, with the mass of American deaths fueling people's quest to connect with their deceased loved ones.[21]

Over the years, the fascination with the board simply grew. Remarkably, Parker Brothers sold 2 million Ouija boards in 1967 after the company bought the game, and decades earlier in 1944—a time of international strife—one department store is said to have sold fifty thousand units.[22]

But why has the board lived on and maintained its place in culture? Murch has argued that the 1973 movie *The Exorcist* transformed how people view the Ouija board. While previous films joked about the board, the terrifying cinematic story about a girl who became possessed after using the device absolutely "terrified America."[23]

Joseph P. Laycock, a professor of religious studies at Texas State University, agreed that it was the film and the novel it was based on that "cemented the Ouija board's sinister reputation in the popular imagination."[24]

"The Ouija board developed out of Spiritualism, a 19th-century movement known for its optimistic views about the future and the afterlife," Laycock wrote. "As Spiritualism's popularity waned, the Ouija board emerged as a popular parlor game; it was only in the 20th century that the Catholic Church and the horror movie industry rebranded the game as a doorway to the demonic."[25]

Laycock noted, though, that the Catholic Church had already spent decades warning people against the use of the Ouija board. And it should also be mentioned that there were bizarre stories surrounding the board well before Hollywood delivered *The Exorcist*. Just consider the strange 1929 murder case involving two women named Nancy Bowen, 66, and Lila Jimerson, 36, who purportedly turned to a Ouija board to try and find out why Bowen's husband, Charlie Bowen, had died.[26]

As the story goes, the board revealed the words, "They killed me," and then the name "Clothilde" emerged, along with an address and a description of the purported murderer.[27] Thus, Bowen, over time, became convinced that a local woman named Clothilde Marchand killed her husband, and so she eventually headed to the woman's home . . . and killed her. The *New York Daily News* explained:

And so it was on March 7, 1930, that Mrs. Marchand, a petit painter who set aside a promising career to raise four children, answered

117

a knock and was confronted by a stranger who accused her in broken English of being a witch.

Nancy Bowen pulled a hammer and beat down the Frenchwoman, then finished the job by stuffing chloroform-soaked paper down her throat.[28]

Bizarrely, Bowen said during her trial that she had tried to kill the woman with hexes, but when that failed, she made the grisly decision. A lot of other bizarre details unfolded, with the revelation that Jimerson was apparently having an affair with Marchand before the murder.

Eventually, Jimerson was freed, and Bowen pleaded guilty to manslaughter and was given time served, but the case itself—and the involvement of the Ouija board—became an absolute sensation.

SCIENCE AND THE OUIJA BOARD

Not everyone is convinced the Ouija board can connect people to the spiritual realm. Some believe there's a perfectly good explanation for what's unfolding on the board—the apparent moving of the planchette.

Scott G. Eberle wrote an opinion piece on the topic in 2012, noting that the Ouija board's success and interest depends on two specific factors—things he said are neither "a secret" nor "arising from malign spirits."[29]

In addition to writing about the suspension of disbelief as people play the game, Eberle also spoke of a "clever deception in manipulating the planchette."[30] He said there are often open secrets that everyone playing the game is aware of, and that players who know one another might then push toward the aspiration they assume a person wants.

But his theory doesn't end there, as he spoke of the notion of "ideomotor action," an idea introduced by British physiologist William Benjamin Carpenter back in the mid-1800s. Eberle explained how the theory works:

Here's how ideomotor action works. The planchette may seem to drag our hands along as it selects letters that spell out words, but it happens that muscular action does not always arise out of deliberate will or volition or, in fact, even upon our awareness. Our keen expectations for a certain outcome will sometimes direct the movements of our arms and hands as the planchette glides easily on felt-covered feet. This happens at a level that lies below our conscious attention. "Dousing" sticks or "divining" rods, which also appear to move strangely on their own, work in exactly this way by amplifying muscle movements.

Whether we're looking for buried pipes or for answers, though, subtle, unacknowledged suggestions, not spirits, guide our actions. Yes, we select the letters ourselves in this game; it's just that sometimes we don't quite know that we do it—or how we do it.[31]

Others share similar perspectives. *Vox* writer Aja Romano, who penned a 2018 article promising that Ouija boards "won't actually put you in contact with demons or spirits," delivered a perspective on how these "talking boards" work.[32]

Like Eberle, Romano described the ideomotor effect as "a way for your body to talk to itself." These involuntary movements are said to be unconscious and come even as we're trying not to move our hands, with Romano comparing the dynamic to what happens when a person jerks or moves in his or her sleep. These involuntary movements happen at an unconscious level, she argued.

Romano continues: "In the case of a Ouija board, your brain may unconsciously create images and memories when you ask the board questions. Your body responds to your brain without you consciously 'telling' it to do so, causing the muscles in your hands and arms to move the pointer to the answers that you—again, unconsciously—may want to receive."[33]

Eberle and others have suggested that a simple blindfold test disproves any spiritual elements of the Ouija board.[34] Their contention? If you blindfold someone and tilt the board, he or she suddenly won't be able to spell any words. And, if this is the case—and if spellings are dependent on the ability to see the board—these critics argue that it's clearly an act of one's own mind and not a spiritual or demonic force moving the planchette.

Before his eerie death, even Fuld reportedly had his own skepticism about the product he was successfully selling. "Believe in the Ouija board? I should say not," he reportedly once said. "I'm no spiritualist. I'm a Presbyterian—been one ever since I was so high."[35]

Other researchers have specifically explored the Ouija board and have come away with similar results. Still, people around the world report inexplicable phenomena that they believe is directly tied to their use of the board.

Are they lying, delusional, or simply imagining what's unfolding? Many faith leaders would affirm that these people are telling the truth—and that severe caution is a must. Brown said he believes it's better to avoid the Ouija board altogether, again appealing to his past experience speaking with people who have dabbled in the occult.

"Ask the people that came out of Satanism, ask the people that came out of witchcraft, ask the people that were really demonically bound if it's okay to play around with Ouija boards or tarot cards or things like that," he said. "And I would say, universally they'll say: 'Don't touch them.'"

9

Do Ghosts Really Exist?

The overarching discussion about demons, possession, and, in particular, infestation lends itself to another interesting topic of discussion: ghosts. Defined simply as "a disembodied soul," ghosts are generally believed by some to be deceased human beings whose spirits somehow remain here on Earth.[1]

This is an entirely different concept from demons, which are expressly discussed throughout the New Testament narrative. Ghosts are not given much attention if any at all in the Scriptures—especially not with the prevalence of demons, possession, and exorcism.

But are they real? Some would answer affirmatively, and there are certainly scores of spiritual practitioners and so-called ghost hunters around the globe who devote a plethora of their time to trying to prove, monitor, and expose ghosts' existence.

Meanwhile, psychics and mediums pledge to help grieving people reach deceased loved ones from beyond the grave (a practice known as necromancy)—a dynamic that mirrors the ways in which the Ouija board is often used. The belief among these individuals and those who seek them is that it is possible to conjure the spirit of a deceased person in an effort to connect or speak to that individual from beyond the grave.

Whether this is possible or not is a subject of intense debate, but the quest to connect with the dead is certainly a timeless practice that has been unfolding for thousands of years. So, where does the public stand on the existence of ghosts? As I shared earlier in this book, polling shows that 45 percent of adult Americans admit to believing in ghosts, with 43 percent revealing that they believe ghosts can haunt either places or people.[2]

But that's not the only statistic that stands out. The well-respected Pew Research Center found in 2009 that a substantial proportion of American adults reported having had a personal experience involving a "ghost."[3] "Nearly one in five U.S. adults (18%) say they've seen or been in the presence of a ghost," the Pew report read. "An even greater share—29%— say they have felt in touch with someone who has already died."[4]

> *Forty-five percent of adult Americans admit to believing in ghosts.*

Those are some pretty stunning statistics, as a notable proportion of people believe they have had some sort of experience in this arena. And while we don't have much data on these beliefs or experiences before 2009, we do know that, throughout the millennia, the concept of ghosts has both captivated and terrified many people across the globe.

As mentioned, Hollywood has tapped into this seemingly endless intrigue over the spiritual realm, jumping on the bandwagon to create TV shows and films on the topic. From horror movies to reality shows that include investigators looking for ghosts and mediums connecting with the dead, there's no shortage of ghost-themed content. Likewise, ghosts get a fair amount of attention during the Halloween season each year.

But what's the truth of the matter? Is it possible, scripturally speaking, for human spirits to remain behind after death and to haunt, or do people simply go to heaven or hell after they leave their bodies, completely disconnecting from the earthly realm?

These curiosities are fascinating and timeless, though there does seem to be a bit of a consensus among Christians and, as we'll explore, there's a scriptural reason for a solid level of uniformity on the ghost front.

Evangelicals, in particular, generally reject the notion that someone would die and come back or remain on Earth to haunt. Emily McFarlan Miller captured this sentiment in a piece for *Relevant* when she wrote, "The overwhelming preponderance of evangelical experts say the Christian worldview does not allow for ghosts haunting the Earth."[5]

Miller went on to note that almost every denomination under the Christian umbrella agrees with the following: "Any spirit that is not God is not to be trifled with" and that one should not seek out the deceased.[6]

But while there seems to be at least a majority Christian view against the existence of ghosts, not everyone with a biblical worldview is in total agreement. Like so many of the other most common theological questions, various groups under the Christian umbrella have divergent perspectives on the matter.

As theology website GotQuestions.org notes:

Within the Christian faith, there is a significant amount of confusion regarding what happens after death. Some hold that after death, everyone "sleeps" until the final judgment, after which everyone will be sent to heaven or hell. Others believe that at the moment of death, people are instantly judged and sent to their eternal destinations. Still others claim that when people die, their souls/spirits are sent to a "temporary" heaven or hell, to await the final resurrection, the final judgment, and then the finality of their eternal destination.[7]

I decided to more deeply explore these views to see what a wide swath of practicing Christians have to say on the matter. And, as expected, a survey among Christians commissioned through HarperCollins Consumer Insights in preparation for publishing *Playing with Fire* found that the vast majority of Christians polled (75 percent) rejected the notion that a person who dies can remain behind and haunt a location.

Meanwhile, 8 percent said such hauntings are possible, and 17 percent expressed being unsure; the proportions were similar among church leaders.

While this data is intriguing, I want to make another note about the 2009 Pew data that found nearly one in five US adults claiming they had seen or been in the presence of a ghost: churchgoers were much less likely to report experiencing such a dynamic. Pew explains:

> Does going to church help keep ghosts away? It's impossible to say, but people who often go to worship services appear to be less likely to say they see ghosts. Just 11% of those who attend religious services at least weekly say they've been in the presence of a ghost, while 23% of those who attend services less frequently say they have seen a ghost, the Pew Research Center survey found.[8]

There's much to unpack here, but one of the central theories that emerges is if everything humans report seeing or experiencing is actually demonic in nature as some experts contend, then it seems noteworthy that churchgoers—people who have no problem embracing the existence of the spiritual realm—would report fewer experiences with ghosts.

It's clearly not a stretch to assume that churchgoers are more likely than the general public to be genuinely faithful, authentic Christians and are, thus, less likely to dabble in the occult or partake in actions that would conjure up the spiritual issues we've discussed in this book.

If one embraces the belief that ghosts are an impossibility and that spiritual issues stem from the demonic, then it would make sense for Christians to have a lower rate of inviting in and, thus, experiencing these spiritual influences.

Author Ron Rhodes tackled this in his book, *The Truth Behind Ghosts, Mediums, and Psychic Phenomena*, when he said some mistakenly believe they have encountered ghosts when, in reality, they have communed with something far more sinister.

It seems noteworthy that churchgoers—people who have no problem embracing the existence of the spiritual realm—would report fewer experiences with ghosts.

"People sometimes genuinely encounter a spirit entity—though not a dead human," Rhodes wrote. "Some people encounter demonic spirits who may mimic dead people in order to deceive the living (see 1 John 4:1; 1 Timothy 4:1–3). Many who claim to have encountered such spirit entities have some prior involvement in the occult."[9]

If we back up a bit, it's clear that one's beliefs about what happens after death will have a direct and implicit impact on what he or she thinks about the potential existence of ghosts.

There are some specific verses that seem to point to the idea that a person ends up in heaven or hell immediately after death.[10] Second Corinthians 5:8 reads, "We are confident, I say, and would prefer to be away from the body and at home with the Lord." A baseline reading of the text appears to indicate that once Christians are away from our bodies we are with God.

There's also Hebrews 9:27, which reads, "Just as people are destined to die once, and after that to face judgment . . ."—yet another verse some take to indicate an immediate ascent or descent into heaven or hell.

But then we see other verses, like Revelation 20:11–15, which seem to point to a future judgment of the dead:

> Then I saw a great white throne and him who was seated on it. The earth and the heavens fled from his presence, and there was no place for them. And I saw the dead, great and small, standing before the throne, and books were opened. Another book was opened, which is the book of life. The dead were judged according to what they had done as recorded in the books. The sea gave up the dead that were in it, and death and Hades gave up the dead that were in them, and each person was judged according to what they had done. Then death and Hades were thrown into the lake of fire. The lake of fire is the second death. Anyone whose name was not found written in the book of life was thrown into the lake of fire.

In other places, we see simultaneous themes of "sleep" and a call for Jesus to immediately receive someone's spirit. In Acts 7:59–60 when Stephen was being stoned, the martyr proclaimed the following during the horrific experience: "Lord Jesus, receive my spirit."

After Stephen fell on his knees and begged God to "not hold this sin against" those who were killing him, the Bible tells us that "he fell asleep."

We see this theme of sleep emerge in other verses as well. First Thessalonians 4:14 reads, "For we believe that Jesus died and rose again, and so we believe that God will bring with Jesus those who have fallen asleep in him."

And 1 Corinthians 15:17–18 proclaims, "And if Christ has not been raised, your faith is futile; you are still in your sins. Then those also who have fallen asleep in Christ are lost."

The notion that there is immediate afterlife is quite common and seems to be embedded in Scripture, though there are those who embrace the idea that humans essentially fall into a spiritual sleep while "awaiting the second coming and the judgment."[11]

The aforementioned verses speak into that dynamic, but famed pastor and theologian John Piper is among those who believe that people do not fall into an unconscious sleep for eons until Jesus' return. He appealed to Paul in an explainer on the topic, noting that the apostle said that he would "gain" after death by being in Christ's presence (Philippians 1:21–23).

"So when Paul contemplates his own dying, he calls it 'gain,' not because he is going to go unconscious and have zero experience for another thousand years, but because he goes into the presence of Christ with Christ in a deeper, more intimate way," Piper proclaimed. "And it is, he says, vastly better than anything he has known here."[12]

And the theologian again pointed to Paul in 2 Corinthians 5:6–9 to note that Paul proclaimed that when we are "away from the body" we are "at home with the Lord." Piper concluded: "Dying in the body means going to be at home with the Lord."[13]

There are other verses we could explore, but for the sake of brevity we will only dive into one more—and it's perhaps the most intriguing biblical proclamation about death. The thought-provoking moment unfolds when Christ was on the cross talking to one of the criminals who was crucified next to him. We learn in Luke 23 that one of the criminals hurled insults at Jesus and said, "Aren't you the Messiah? Save yourself and us!" (v. 39).

But the other criminal rebuked him and said, "Don't you fear God?" before noting that the two of them were "punished justly" for their deeds, but that Christ had done nothing wrong (vv. 40–41). It's the dialogue that comes next—Jesus offering forgiveness to the criminal—that speaks into this overarching death debate.

Criminal: "Jesus, remember me when you come into your kingdom."

Jesus: "Truly I tell you, today you will be with me in paradise." (vv. 42–43)

It is telling that Jesus promised the criminal that he would be with him "in paradise" that very day. This dialogue is quite compelling and seems to be speaking about an immediate departure to a heavenly state. Still, some have found other ways of interpreting its meaning, believing, instead, that Christians remain in a sleep state until Christ's eventual return.

SO, WHAT DOES THE BIBLE SAY ABOUT GHOSTS?

Though the Scriptures aren't completely ironclad mum on the issue, one could argue that the near-silence on ghosts speaks volumes. Let's explore a few places where some might argue that ghosts can be seen in the Scriptures. Matthew 27, and verses 52–53 in particular, is a section of Scripture that boldly stood out while researching this book.

We see a number of stunning occurrences in Matthew 27 both before and after Christ's death, including a darkness that "came over all the land" right before Jesus' spirit left his body (v. 45).

And after Jesus cried out and gave up his spirit we see some additional lines of text that should give us pause—scriptures that seem to point to what some might see as a ghostly scenario. Verses 51–54 read:

At that moment the curtain of the temple was torn in two from top to bottom. The earth shook, the rocks split and the tombs broke open. *The bodies of many holy people who had died were raised to life. They came out of the tombs after Jesus' resurrection and went into the holy city and appeared to many people.* When the centurion and those with him who were guarding Jesus saw the earthquake and all that had happened, they were terrified, and exclaimed, "Surely he was the Son of God!" (emphasis added)

These verses are stunning. What exactly is unfolding here when the bodies of people who had died come back to life—and suddenly appear to "many"?

First and foremost, it's important to note that these events unfolded after the most transformational event in human history; so, to assume that this was or is some sort of norm would be an improper approach. Still, the fact that it is recorded as happening must be discussed in the context of this overarching ghost conversation.

Piper addressed this scenario in an article on DesiringGod.org titled, "Split Rocks, Open Tombs, Raised Bodies," noting that Christ's death ushered in a number of events—happenings that he believes have specific and important meanings.

Matthew clearly emphasized that Jesus' death opened the tombs and gave new life, as Piper noted. This is reflective of what Christ has done for all of humanity, and it speaks into the deeper meaning of Jesus' resurrection. The theologian further explained:

It seems to me that Matthew is showing us the foundational and essential power of the death of Jesus as the cause of resurrection life in natural bodies, while affirming the Pauline truth that the resurrection of Jesus is also necessary for the full public experience of our physical resurrection—bodies raised at Jesus's death, bodies out of the tombs and into the city at Jesus's resurrection.[14]

Others take similar perspectives. Writing for InTouch Ministries, John Greco said the following about this incredible moment: "These risen disciples served as witnesses to Christ's power over death and His claim to be the Jewish Messiah."[15]

We can only speculate as to why these men and women were allowed to resurrect, but we can be certain it was a unique moment in human and biblical history. Taking it as some sort of example of the existence of ghosts would seem imprudent, though, as it seems specifically tied to Jesus' death and resurrection.

Another particularly interesting piece of scripture unfolds when Jesus was famously walking on water in Matthew 14. Verses 25–26 read, "Shortly before dawn Jesus went out to them [the disciples], walking on the lake. When the disciples saw him walking on the lake, they were terrified."

We're then told that the disciples "cried out in fear" and proclaimed, "It's a ghost." Similar language is observed in the telling of the same story in Mark 6:49–50 when we are told that the disciples "thought he was a ghost" and "cried out" in terror.

The assumption based on these verses is that the disciples were at least aware enough of the concepts of hauntings to assume—and be simultaneously terrified by—the shocking image of Jesus walking on water.

There's another story involving Jesus where the Bible uses the word *ghost*, and it unfolds in Luke 24:36–39 after Christ's death and resurrection. It is in these verses that we see Jesus suddenly standing before the disciples—a shocking moment considering his crucifixion and death.

After Jesus said, "Peace be with you," we're again told that they were terrified. "They were startled and frightened, thinking they saw a ghost. He said to them, 'Why are you troubled, and why do doubts rise in your minds?'" verses 37–38 read, with verse 39 continuing, "Look at my hands and my feet. It is I myself! Touch me and see; a ghost does not have flesh and bones, as you see I have."

None of this indicates a definitive view that the disciples saw Jesus as a deceased person coming back from the dead. Even if they did believe he was a ghost in the denotative sense, the Bible does not openly lend itself to claiming that this sort of dynamic is normally possible or routine.

Then there is another portion of Scripture that I mentioned a bit earlier in this book: the intentional summoning of Samuel by King Saul in 1 Samuel 28. What's most compelling about this scripture is that it is, according to GotQuestions.org, "the only biblical account of someone being visited by someone who was deceased."[16]

One could also mention the Transfiguration in Matthew 17—the moment Moses and Elijah appear and talk to Jesus—as another potential ghostly encounter. Elijah, who the Bible says didn't die and was instead taken to heaven, wouldn't qualify, but Moses, who had died, would. Still, again, this seems to be a powerful moment that is specifically connected to Christ and would seem to be a special circumstance.

Either way, let's get back to Saul's experience. Following the prophet Samuel's death, Saul had expelled all of the mediums from Israel. But when Saul found himself terrified and up against the Philistines, he was overtaken by fear.

After driving himself entirely away from the Lord, Saul saught out a medium in a desperate attempt to reach Samuel from beyond the grave, telling the spirit channeler, "I am in great distress. . . . The Philistines are fighting against me, and God has departed from me. He no longer answers me, either by prophets or by dreams. So I have called on you to tell me what to do" (1 Samuel 28:15).

This mirrors the desperation some experience in the wake of losing a loved one, or when overtaken by the weight of uncertainty about the future. It's why so many people turn to psychics and mediums in the first place, and we can see this same desperation and waywardness in Saul's own experience.

The woman agreed to try and reach Samuel, but what the deceased prophet revealed when he appeared did little to make Saul feel better. Samuel proclaimed: "The LORD will deliver both Israel and you into the hands of the Philistines, and tomorrow you and your sons will be with me. The LORD will also give the army of Israel into the hands of the Philistines" (v. 19).

It seems, from the text, that Samuel was potentially success-fully reached from beyond the grave, but, again, there's nothing in the Bible that tells us this sort of conjuring is normal, routine, or typical. It's quite possible God simply allowed Samuel to be seen in an effort to deliver Saul's fate. There are also other theories, includ-ing this one about demonic influence that was recapped by Answers in Genesis:

> However, this [Samuel] passage doesn't suggest that séances work, and it absolutely doesn't condone witchcraft. Some scholars believe that God sent Samuel on this unique occasion. But others believe a demon was impersonating the prophet based on the fact that he made some false claims. For example, commentator John Gill notes that the apparition warned that all of Saul's sons would die on the next day, but some survived.[17]

Based strictly on facts in the text, there's not much more we can definitively say about the encounter. At the least, it's an intriguing moment in biblical history worthy of exploration. So, let's get back to the broader discussion: the existence of ghosts. Some of the experts and pastors I consulted for this book were adamant about their belief that ghosts as presented in popular culture—the spirits of departed human beings—simply do not exist.

And if these alleged apparitions aren't people, we're forced to answer another question: What are they?

"I personally do not believe it's humans," Chad Norris, senior pastor at Bridgeway Church in Greenville, South Carolina, told me. "I believe it is the evil realm. . . . I do not believe that it's people. That's my opinion."

Dr. Shane Wood offered a fascinating explanation when asked if it's possible for a person's spirit to remain, noting that he believes human beings often underestimate "the amount of mystery and . . . power" that unfolds when people cross over into the afterlife.

"When you're talking about the amount of power and energy that is contained in a soul and when it is released or breaks the veil between heaven and Earth, I don't know that we really appreciate the significance of that moment and the power that it contains," he said.

Regardless of speculation and debate over the idea or reality of real-life ghosts and hauntings, Wood made a related argument about the demonic realm that he and other experts believe is essential to this discussion. "It's a key tactic of demons to pretend to be someone that has died in order to gain more permission," he said. "If it is . . . an entity that's claiming to be a person that's haunting, you need to treat it as the worst-case scenario. You need to treat it as a demon."

The key takeaway from this discussion is that the Bible definitively tells us there is a spiritual war unfolding and that Satan and his minions exist; the Bible does not, however, speak to the notion that people die and remain behind to haunt. Even in the case of Samuel, he needed to be summoned, and considering the events surrounding Saul and his decision to turn from God, the argument that the Lord simply allowed this contact—an incredibly narrow and rare act—is logically appealing.

We do not see these sorts of ghostly events unfolding in radical form throughout Scripture, though we do see the impact of demons and the need for expulsion making routine appearances throughout the New Testament.

People might dismiss the entire discussion about demons and ghosts, but based on a reading of the contents of Scripture, this seems to be the most logical literary takeaway.

As we explore the biblical narrative, we must also reexamine the ways in which exorcisms and healings presented in Scripture translate to the modern era. This requires understanding the ins and outs of both exorcism and deliverance, and the contemporary methods by which these processes are carried out.

PART FOUR

RELEASE FROM THE DEMONIC

10

EXORCISM AND DELIVERANCE

I never saw any of this coming for me, Billy. I didn't see any of it coming."

By all accounts, Chad Norris, senior pastor at Bridgeway Church in Greenville, South Carolina, is a normal guy. He's married, has three kids, enjoys sports—and loves Jesus.

"There's nothing fancy about me," he said during an interview for this book.

Still, there is something quite *fascinating* about Norris. He's among the pastors and faith leaders who have helped those claiming to be afflicted by the demonic, and he's apparently seen thousands of spiritual struggles unfold over the years.

Norris's own foray into this realm took root at a Texas summer camp years ago when he said he personally observed multiple voices coming from a girl believed to be afflicted by the demonic. "The first thing that happened to me is the most dramatic thing that I've seen in twenty years," Norris said of his experience in this realm. "And that's saying a lot."

His journey touched off after he prayed one day to God when he was a youth camp pastor at Angelo State University in San Angelo, Texas, in his early twenties. Norris told the Lord that he wanted to see the "stories in the Gospels" come alive—the healings, miracles, and castings out of demons that are embedded in the biblical text.

Norris wanted to experience these truths in his life and ministry, telling God he was ready and willing to jump into the fray. "I don't care what it cost me," Norris told God. "I want to do everything You did." He said everything changed for him the very day that prayer was uttered.

Norris received a jarring phone call from the head of the camp, who said, "Chad, do you have any experience in demon delivery?" The young preacher answered affirmatively, though he actually wasn't very well versed in deliverance or exorcisms. "I would have never said yes if I knew what was about to happen," he recalled.

Norris remembers entering a room not long after and encountering a sixteen-year-old girl who was clearly experiencing something traumatic—something he had never seen before. "It was so demonic in the atmosphere, you could feel it," he said. "I knew something was wrong."

Norris prayed and then looked at the young woman and said, "In the name of Jesus, I command whoever is bothering this young lady . . . to tell me who you are." The response, which he said came in plural voices, shot back in "a loud, gargling voice."

"We are Nephilim," the voices barked.

The startling moment left Norris in shock. Unfortunately, the attempted deliverance didn't amount to anything; he lost track of the student and isn't sure whether she was ever healed. But the unharmonious encounter was the true starting point of Norris's understanding of spiritual warfare and his path forward into the ministry. "Twenty years later, I've seen perhaps even thousands of things since then," he said. "That first encounter . . . it scared me, but it made me go, 'What else do I not know?'"

Norris's account is hardly rare, with many others sharing similar stories. Those who doubt the existence of the demonic might not realize that there's a vast and active spiritual world out there filled with Christians who are engaged in fighting against perceived evils. There are solidified processes comprised of specific remedies through which Christian faith leaders will try to help those who believe they've been afflicted in some way by diabolical, spiritual forces.

These efforts, which generally differ depending on Christian faith traditions, typically come in the form of exorcism or deliverance, and I'll dive into some of the finer elements in this chapter. But before we explore more intensely what these spiritual battles look like, definitions matter—and in this conversation, the terms used by various Christian leaders can be complex or confusing, especially considering changing contexts and circumstances.

The confounding nature of the discussion is further perpetuated by the cultural lens through which Hollywood movies present the demonic. Films and TV shows tend to universally present these issues and scenes as incredibly chaotic, showing priests and pastors screaming, tossing holy water, and engaging in overtly physical battles with demonic forces and the afflicted themselves.

But when you research and speak with those who work in this realm, it seems the real-life handling of these issues can look quite different from the big screen's portrayal. Father Gary Thomas, a longtime exorcist in the Catholic Church, is among those who have spoken out about what Hollywood gets right—and wrong—about exorcisms and deliverance. He said the efforts sometimes made to investigate and heal those impacted by the demonic are not given the deserved airtime.

"The ministry of exorcism and deliverance is a ministry of healing," he told a priests' convention in 2017. "It is not the drama of Hollywood, although there is drama. This is primarily a ministry of healing. We have a responsibility as [a] church to provide pastoral care."[1]

It's not shocking to consider that many theologians and pastors likely believe the breadth and depth of the spiritual issues experienced by human beings are not adequately presented in Hollywood films. Still, it's an issue that must be mentioned and briefly explored. After all, the most popular cultural explorations of these issues—like many other cultural phenomena—tend to be through entertainment; thus it is important that we dig a bit deeper into the mix to understand exactly what terms like *exorcism* and *deliverance* mean and how they manifest in tangible and spiritual form.

Reverend Benjamin McEntire, an Anglican priest in the Communion of Evangelical Episcopal Churches and an Alaska Air National Guard chaplain who has spent his career working in the spiritual warfare realm, has addressed the differences in language used to describe possession and spiritual healing. "Different groups use different labels, but sometimes they will use the exact same word but mean different things by it," he told me.

Speaking specifically about *exorcism*, he said this is a term that could also mean "advanced deliverance"—something that happens in extreme and intense scenarios when a person is believed to have been overtaken by a demonic spirit. "It's going to be a rather rare case where the demonic has such a hold on a person, and their will is so weakened, it's been so eroded by the enemy that they're not really able to participate in the process at all," he said. "So it requires this back and forth between weakening the enemy's hold and working to strengthen the person's will."

Dr. Shane Wood agreed with this definition and said that his own research has led him to believe that "actual, full-blown possession is incredibly rare" due to its nature and impact. "What full-blown possession is, is basically the complete suppression of the will of the host," he said. "It's to the point where they have so given their will over completely . . . [they have] granted permission so thoroughly that the demon can be fully present at all moments or any moment it decides."

Deliverance is another term that is frequently used in the spiritual warfare space, with McEntire framing it as any process in which the afflicted person "is able to actively engage in the process the entire time." Others have also weighed in over the years to offer similar differentiators.

The late legendary psychiatrist Dr. M. Scott Peck, who died in 2005, distinguished between exorcism and deliverance in a similar way, calling the latter "a brief procedure and a gentle one that can be done without restraints." He said it should be done with two people and can happen during a single afternoon.

"It's very quiet and peaceful, mostly people just praying, and as the delivery progresses it becomes obvious that there is a problem that sometimes can be taken care of . . . by simply identifying some kind of demonic presence and ordering it out," he said in a 2005 interview with *Salon*. "It's all very peaceful and easy and simple."[2]

Deliverance in itself (different from "advanced deliverance") is more of a prayerful approach to tackling spiritual warfare and affliction; it is not the same as a full exorcism and is something many people go through in an effort to overcome personal struggles or spiritual afflictions in their lives. We'll deal more with this topic later in this chapter, but Peck offered an analogy once given by Dr. Francis MacNutt, an expert on deliverance, that might help us more diligently understand the finer points when it comes to the difference between deliverance and exorcism.

"Oppression is like a city where the enemy has gotten hold of a couple of suburbs but does not in any way control the whole city," Peck said. "As far as possession, [MacNutt] describes it as a city where the city center and the radio stations and roadways have all been captured by the enemy, and you need a massive onslaught to get the enemy out of there, and that's an exorcism."[3]

Others have different ways of tackling these terms, with the Catholic Church taking a definitive and pointed approach—one that is uniform and multifaceted.

How Catholics Tackle Exorcism

Catholics are known for exorcism ceremonies that the Vatican believes will help lead people toward spiritual healing. The United States Conference of Catholic Bishops (USCCB) describes exorcism in a way that might seem surprising to some, dubbing it "a specific form of prayer that the Church uses against the power of the devil."[4]

It is this prayer effort, according to Catholics, that underpins and constitutes the basis of any exorcism attempt, with the effort being undertaken to try and free a person from spiritual oppression—something Catholics have systematically practiced for hundreds of years.

"There are instances when a person needs to be protected against the power of the devil or to be withdrawn from his spiritual domin-ion," the USCCB explains. "At such times, the Church asks publicly and authoritatively in the name of Jesus Christ for this protection or liberation through the use of exorcism."[5]

The Catholic Church first issued its guidance on exorcisms in 1614, with the Vatican making international headlines in 1999 when officials decided to make the first amendments in centuries to the eighty-four-page document titled, *De Exorcismis et Supplicationibus Quibusdam* ("Of Exorcisms and Certain Supplications").

The guidance document was slightly amended again in 2004.[6] This 1999 move, though, was noteworthy for a variety of reasons—mainly because it drove home the Catholic Church's belief in Satan's existence and his "work in the world," as the *New York Times* noted.[7] The rite of Catholic exorcism is in Latin, so a separate decision in 2014 by the USCCB to adopt an English version—and the latter approval of this move by the Vatican—was another big deal, with the words being spoken aloud during an exorcism suddenly able to be understood by an afflicted person who is unversed in Latin.[8]

One of the major clarifications to the practice was an increased emphasis on the importance of differentiating between mental and spiritual issues—something the *Times* said was doubled down on in "an apparent effort to placate liberal Catholics embarrassed by a practice that seems to echo medieval superstition."[9] The text of the revised rite warns to "not consider people to be vexed by demons who are suffering above all from some psychic illness."[10] We will explore mental-health concerns in a later chapter, as it is an essential component of the discussion and one that leads to the biggest critiques of exorcism and deliverance.

But for the purposes of this chapter, let's further explore the definitions associated with this discussion. The Catholic Church recognizes two types of exorcism: minor and major. The first is used for and relates to those preparing to be baptized, among other spiritual activities, and its purpose is to offer prayer that is intended to help a person overcome evil or sin in his or her life. Minor exorcisms are used for the Rite of Christian Initiation of Adults—the process through which an adult converts to the Catholic faith, or when children are baptized. This is essentially uniform and standard theological fare for helping protect people against evil.[11]

It is the second type of exorcism, though—the major exorcism—that most people are familiar with, as major exorcisms are intended to expel demons and remove a person from the throes of possession.[12] The "Of Exorcisms and Certain Supplications" document that governs exorcisms contains an introduction and two chapters, with the first covering the rite of exorcism and the second exploring additional texts on the matter.

One of the key differences between the Catholic Church and other Christian denominations is the system surrounding who is permitted or called to perform an exorcism. Catholics hold the belief that the process must be carried out by a priest or bishop with permission from the diocese. But many Christians from the nondenominational realm and other Protestant traditions believe that any Christian, through the name of Christ, has authority to expel evil. It is the name of Christ, alone, many non-Catholics believe, that holds the power to overtake and drive out evil.

As for Catholics, though, priests go through training before entering into the exorcism vocation. And if there's any confusion about the lines drawn between who should and shouldn't be performing exorcisms, the USCCB openly issues caution for any layperson who might decide to engage in the rite of exorcism.

"The text cautions that the lay faithful are not to recite any prayers reserved to the exorcist, not only because the prayers are reserved to those ordained to act in the person of Christ the Head (in persona Christi capitis), but also to protect the faithful from possible spiritual harm," a USCCB explainer reads.[13]

The subject of who is deemed qualified to perform an exorcism is without a doubt one of the most pointed conflicts on this matter among different Christian denominations. For Catholics, the clergy rule is strict and uniform. Consider the fact that only bishops reportedly have access to the English-language translation of the rite, though priests and others engaged in this realm can have access with permission from the bishop.[14] Others outside of the Catholic realm take divergent approaches.

"Training an exorcist varies extensively by one's tradition. Not every Christian group who affirms exorcism as a legitimate and needed ministry believes in appointing exorcists, with many of those seeing 'possession' as being so rare that one cannot train for it," McEntire told me. "Others use the term 'deliverance' instead of 'exorcism' and have an entirely different understanding of the ministry."

The people in this latter group typically don't have any exorcists-in-training. But when it comes to those who do indeed believe in the need for appointing exorcists, training is typically implicit—and Catholics are the best example of this dynamic.

"Often no formal training process exists for Protestant exorcists," McEntire said.

We'll leave the training discussion there, though the diversity in approach again speaks to the complexity of the understanding of these spiritual issues. Let's circle back to the degree to which people must strategize and institutionalize an exorcism versus simply relying on Jesus' name to expel the demonic.

"The Catholic rite is very structured, whereas some of the other churches are more creative," Pedro Barrajón, a Catholic priest involved in organizing an annual exorcism-training event at the Vatican, told the *Telegraph*. "They don't use a precise format."[15]

As part of that format, Catholics appeal to the use of holy water, the sign of the cross, or a crucifix (or cross) to help drive out evil—elements that are many times not included by Protestants working in the same realm. The USCCB explains the "sacred symbols" included in the Catholic exorcism rite:

> In addition to the use of the Psalms and Gospel readings and the recitation of the exorcistic prayers, a series of sacred symbols is utilized in the Rite of Major Exorcism. To begin, water is blessed and sprinkled recalling the centrality of the new life the afflicted person received in Baptism and the ultimate defeat of the devil through the salvific work of Jesus Christ. The imposition of hands, as well as the breathing on the person's face

(exsufflation) by the exorcist, reaffirms the power of the Holy Spirit at work in the person as a result of his/her Baptism, confirming him/her as a temple of God. Finally, the Lord's Cross is shown to the afflicted person and the Sign of the Cross is made over him/her demonstrating the power of Christ over the devil.[16]

The Catholic process is again very uniform and structured, with no priest or bishop deviating from the text of the exorcism rite, and with various religious tools and strategies being employed in the process. Others like McEntire take a middle ground approach to this piece of the exorcism puzzle, noting that the use of various tools like crucifixes and holy water come from a "pretty standard sacramental outlook."

When asked if he has personally observed afflicted persons react to these elements, he answered affirmatively. "My experience has been yes, very often they do—not always, but often. I've seen them react to that type of thing before myself," he said. "I have no problem with that Scripturally as well because we do see some examples in Scripture where God used physical objects as a means to minister to people. The cloths taken from Paul where people found healing and freedom from evil spirits, when they came in contact with those cloths would be one example of that."

McEntire appealed to Acts 19:11–12 when addressing physical objects Paul had touched. "God did extraordinary miracles through Paul," verse 11 reads, with verse 12 continuing, "so that even handkerchiefs and aprons that had touched him were taken to the sick, and their illnesses were cured and the evil spirits left them."

As for his own approach, McEntire said he will sometimes employ physical items but that he uses a "very flexible approach" based on how he feels led, the comfort of the person he is working with, and other ministerial elements.

How Non-Catholics Handle Exorcism and Deliverance

It's clear that McEntire's more fluid approach isn't in lockstep with the Catholic Church. It's also clear that Christians outside of the Catholic realm take vastly different approaches to driving out the demonic. But this hardly encapsulates the entirety of the demonic debate, as some Christians also question whether exorcism is still something the Bible calls us to engage in today.

Christian resource GotQuestions.org, for instance, notes the existence and prevalence of exorcism in the Gospels, but in one article takes a relatively restrained approach to discussing its manifestation in the modern era.[17]

"It appears that the purpose of Jesus' disciples performing exorcisms was to show Christ's dominion over the demons (Luke 10:17) and to verify that the disciples were acting in His name and by His authority. It also revealed their faith or lack of faith (Matthew 17:14–21)," the website reads. "It was obvious that this act of casting out demons was important to the ministry of the disciples. However, it is unclear what part casting out demons actually played in the discipleship process."[18]

The website goes on to note that there "seems to be a shift" in the New Testament after the Gospels and the book of Acts when it comes to issues pertaining to the demonic. While demonic activity is acknowledged throughout New Testament Scriptures, GotQuestions.org notes that the New Testament seems to later pivot to focus more on the importance of standing up against such activity, without stark mentions of casting out demons or instructions on how to do so.

From Romans through Jude, GotQuestions.org contends that the focus is on resisting Satan and following the proclamations in Ephesians 6:11–18, not necessarily actively taking steps to cast out demons. These verses about arming oneself with God's power read:

Put on the full armor of God, so that you can take your stand against the devil's schemes. For our struggle is not against flesh and blood, but against the rulers, against the authorities, against the powers of this dark world and against the spiritual forces of evil in the heavenly realms.

Therefore put on the full armor of God, so that when the day of evil comes, you may be able to stand your ground, and after you have done everything, to stand. Stand firm then, with the belt of truth buckled around your waist, with the breastplate of righteousness in place, and with your feet fitted with the readiness that comes from the gospel of peace.

In addition to all this, take up the shield of faith, with which you can extinguish all the flaming arrows of the evil one. Take the helmet of salvation and the sword of the Spirit, which is the word of God. And pray in the Spirit on all occasions with all kinds of prayers and requests. With this in mind, be alert and always keep on praying for all the Lord's people.[19]

The aforementioned GotQuestions.org article doesn't rule out exorcism and driving out demons but notes that this shift in focus makes it "difficult to determine instructions on how to do such a thing." The article concludes, "If necessary at all, it seems that it is through exposing the individual to the truth of the Word of God and the name of Jesus Christ."[20]

From a purely factual and literary standpoint, it's entirely possible that there is not as much of an active shift in the New Testament as there is a completion of the spiritual narrative surrounding demons. The Gospels and Acts certainly take a deep look at how Christ and his followers approached the demonic, and the remaining instructive books in the New Testament focus instead on prevention and spiritual health.

Looking through this lens, you have one portion of the New

Testament revealing how to deal with possession, and in the other you have a deeper focus on how—through the shield of Christ—one can take preventative steps to stop spiritual issues from unfolding in our lives.

So, what do others in the Christian realm who fully embrace the power of exorcism have to say? Controversial preacher and TV host Pat Robertson, founder of the Christian Broadcasting Network, once offered a brief explainer on demons and exorcism, writing that "exorcism is accomplished by the spoken word, in the name of Jesus, through the power of the Holy Spirit, and it is done simply and quickly."[21]

Under his paradigm, the person performing the exorcism should be a Christian who doesn't have any unrepentant sin, as he said Satan would use any such weaknesses to target the person attempting to expel evil. "This person has to be pure of ulterior motives, sexual impurities, greed, and any other things that might lay him open to some charge by the devil, who is the accuser of the brethren," he wrote.[22]

One of the themes and spiritual warnings important to Robertson as well as the Catholic Church and nearly every expert spoken with for this book: be careful what is attributed to the demonic. Robertson encouraged people not to go seeking demons and not to make false claims about the presence of the demonic.[23]

Be careful what is attributed to the demonic.

But when demonic activity *is* suspected, people like Robertson and McEntire would encourage spiritual remedy. As we've explored, the remedies might differ, but there is general agreement that something must be done to help the afflicted. McEntire offered details about his own process and some of the misconceptions that might unfold due to popular depictions of the demonic. To begin, he dove into the fact that pop culture has led to a general assumption that exorcism is "going to be very violent."

Contrary to the yelling and screaming priests that are sometimes seen spewing in Hollywood films, McEntire—who has presided over at least two full exorcisms and many acts of general deliverance—advocated for a totally different approach. "One of the first things is keeping things calm, steady, stable. That's one of the big parts of this whole process," he said. "Because if a person is coming for ministry—and especially if they think there might be something demonic going on—they have a fear that things are going to get . . . out of control much of the time."

But McEntire said chaotic scenes don't need to unfold, and he also said there isn't always a demonic manifestation (a dramatic event in which a demon makes itself known) in the midst of an exorcism, though he has seen such events happen in certain cases. The centrality of McEntire's view is that he holds the power, through Jesus, to simply command demons not to manifest; he has found this approach effective in his ministry.

And while some might assume only one demon is involved in any purported possession or oppression, McEntire said it is rarely the case that an afflicted person has only one spirit. This belief, he said, impacts how a person approaches a person who is struggling. "One other big thing with this . . . process, though, is that you never, at least in my experience, are dealing with just one demon. You're always dealing with clusters of them," he said. "One of the tactical things a person will benefit from doing is forbidding them from interacting with one another."

McEntire said there are cases he has seen where a deliverance minister is involved in trying to deal with one demon and suddenly another emerges, with these spiritual forces coordinating "their resistance to the process." "By forbidding them to interact and communicate with each other, and also forbidding them to communicate with the person's mind unless they're commanded to do so . . . it really smoothes out the process a lot," he said.

THE MOST IMPORTANT PERSON IN THE ROOM

For more reasons than one, experts agree that the afflicted person is the most essential individual in the room to ensure that healing and ultimate freedom take place. McEntire said demons can try to say no or resist, but that the power to do so really comes from the afflicted person and the legal grounds he or she has given to the spirit (the open door that has enabled the person to be afflicted in the first place).

"If there's still issues within the person that are giving them access, they will usually try to hold on to that and use that as a justification for resisting and not leaving," he said. "That comes down to a, yes, you're acting in the authority of Christ, but at the same time this person is in one sense allowing them permission to stay by not dealing with whatever the issue is that's giving them access."

Peck also offered up an interesting breakdown of the parties involved in exorcism—one worth considering as we attempt to understand the process. People tend to look to faith leaders as the core of any deliverance and exorcism, but Peck agreed that the number-one exorcist who really determines success is the patient.

"The successful end of exorcism, the expulsion of the demon, occurs only when a patient chooses to sever his or her relation with the demonic," he told *Salon*.[24] Peck said the afflicted is the primary success factor, the second is God coming into the room and helping make the exorcism possible, the third is a team of people helping out in the process, and the fourth is the exorcist himself.[25]

The afflicted person must stand at the forefront of healing, but it is also essential for those helping out to have solid biblical worldviews. Bible scholar Dr. Michael Heiser aligns with those working in the field who believe one must "speak truth to lies" in order to stop spiritual oppression, helping the afflicted to see the truth of Jesus as healing takes form.

"You have to have good theology. The solution is truth," he said. "You speak truth to lies. You let that person know, 'Look, Satan is under judgment. This is his fate, and here's how we know. The principalities and powers have no authority. Here's how we know.'"

Norris said that speaking truth into the process is predicated on having a solid spiritual rooting, outlining that there are a number of realities one must be connected with in order to be successful in deliverance ministry. "You have to be so connected in your own heart with receiving love from the Father," he said. "You have to be abiding in that love and that vine because the demonic [realm] . . . cannot stand someone who is truly in love with the Father."

Norris encouraged people to be connected to the Bible, to have faith in the authority that Christians have against the demonic realm, and to have the courage to "pull the trigger" against these forces if and when they are recognized. And Norris said he knows from experience why courage and persistence are essential, sharing another personal example—one that he said was the second most intense demon possession he's ever faced.

Norris was in Cautelas, Haiti, a few years ago, where he said he spent nearly a half-hour trying to deliver a woman who came to him for prayer. "It was very dramatic, but none of it was bothering me because the enemy loves spectacle," he said. "It's such a distraction." In the midst of the deliverance, Norris said he spoke right to the "enemy" and said, "If you do not leave her alone, I am going to torture you." In that moment, he said the woman was "delivered instantly and dramatically."

This showed Norris that passivity isn't beneficial in spiritual warfare, and that grit and reliance on one's faith are essential. He believes deliverance can be delayed or take longer when the person managing it is too passive. "The moment you use that authority and that courage to just not tolerate it, it's really a revelation of the amount of authority we carry," Norris said. "I think most

Christians, if they knew how much authority they carry, it would astound them."

The Coming Together of Forces

Understanding the finer points of exorcism is certainly complex—and those intricacies are even more fascinating when one takes into account the splintering of Christian denominations and leaders over the required tactics to expel evil.

But 2019 brought with it some intriguing developments in this arena, with Christians from different sides of the theological spectrum coming together for the first time to share ideas, tactics, and experiences. This amalgam of religious adherents coalesced in May 2019 at the Vatican's Pontifical Athenaeum Regina Apostolorum when the Catholic Church reportedly decided to open its annual "Course on Exorcism and Prayers of Liberation" to Protestants and others outside the Catholic faith.[26]

The biggest headline from the event is that non-Catholics participated, but the broader curiosity is what was discussed at this gathering that included more than two hundred people who specialize in the spiritual arena.

"Catholics are by no means the only Christians who have developed methods to help possessed people or to rid a space of evil spirits," Father Pedro Barrajón, an exorcist who manages programming at the event, told the *Daily Beast*. "This is the first time we have included so many other religious representatives to share how they do this work. We think collaborating will help us create best practices."[27]

McEntire, who was in attendance, told me that the event tackled a plethora of subject matter relating to exorcism. "The lecture topics included a broad range of technical, theoretical, and some practical subjects," he said. "Some specifics included exorcism and deliverance prayer in Scripture, in Christian tradition, in Catholic canon law, different factors associated with the occult (for example, the occult in the media), psychiatric considerations, various perspectives from other Christian traditions, common phenomena during exorcism, and others."

And there were also geographic considerations, with the event folding in presentations from Latin America, Nigeria, the Philippines, and other localities, with representatives explaining how they train exorcists to tackle issues in these locations. But McEntire explained that the conference "wasn't a practical training course," which is why it was open to people outside of the Catholic faith. He found that it offered "some insightful points" but said that some portions didn't include the wide breadth of opinions and perspectives on spiritual warfare that exist within the Protestant realm.

Only time will tell how the Vatican's decision to bring other Christian practitioners into the fold will impact how various denominations process the attempted expulsion of spiritual evil. The development comes at an interesting time, as some experts warn that perceived incidents of possession and oppression are on the rise.

DEALING WITH DELIVERANCE

What's perhaps most interesting about McEntire's ministry is that the majority of his work in the spiritual warfare arena has been focused on generalized deliverance. Despite presiding over a vast array of deliverances, he has only definitively dealt with two issues of exorcism (also known as advanced deliverance).

"I can't even count the number of deliverances I've done," he said, underscoring the commonality of these spiritual remedies. "That is very routine ministry at this point, so I don't have numbers on it."

It's easy to understand what is claimed to unfold during an

advanced deliverance, but clarity is certainly needed to understand what takes place during a routine deliverance, especially considering the contemporary prevalence of these ministries.

"Probably the biggest difference is that in a deliverance the deliverance is mostly guiding the person through different prayers of repentance, confession, renunciation, of forgiving people that have hurt them in the past," McEntire said. "Of dealing with some of the old hurts of the past. Dealing with lies they've believed about themselves, about God, about others, and experiencing the truth."

A deliverance, he said, is reflective of "prayer-based counseling," though he said a minister might, at moments, command a demon to reveal beliefs or ideals that have been held inside of a person's mind. Others shared similar sentiments. One well-respected and long-standing mental health provider who wished not to be named spoke about his experience with deliverance, offering details about how this form of spiritual healing can benefit patients.

"It's letting [the demons] know that you're not just mouthing these words, 'Be gone in the word of Jesus.' No. You recite Scripture and you recite the prayer," he said. "[And you say], 'You know what? You guys are going to have to bow on your knees and you know your time is short. And you need to just leave this child.'"

Contrary to the Hollywood depiction of exorcism, he said a deliverance is really just a conversation aimed at letting the demonic know it is not welcomed. "It's just a conversation," he said. "It's not this big, huge dramatic thing, at least in my experience, because that wasn't the model that we were given [in the Bible]."

He agreed with Peck that the afflicted person must be willing to renounce the demonic realm, as it was the individual him- or herself who walked through the "doorway" and allowed it to enter in the first place. Additionally, he said it's essential for the afflicted to be rooted in faith.

"The patient has to be able to be willing to close the doorway and repent, because just like the Scripture says, you can sweep it clean, but if you don't fill it back up with something else it comes back sevenfold," he said. "You have to make sure that they're strong in the Lord. The difficulty is that the demons know how to manifest that—they know how to be a fake Christian really well. So . . . you've got to know what you're dealing with."

He went on to share that he always includes another person when conducting a deliverance, and that these spiritual healings are always "prayerfully done." "The patient knows exactly what we're going to do. They've been able to identify the parts of their life that the demonic has influenced," he said. "It's all about getting control back over a certain part of your life, whether it's drugs, alcohol, sex, violence, because demons don't have you do good things to yourself or others."

Notably, McEntire said the people whom he helps through deliverance generally don't realize they need one. "Most of the people I wind up doing deliverance with don't actually believe that they need deliverance," he said. "Usually, they're coming because they have some other type of problem that they've not been able to overcome."

McEntire cited porn addiction as just one of the many examples of an issue someone might struggle with yet not initially see as having spiritual roots. "Very often, part of what's going on there is that there are some evil spirits that are actually using that as a way to hold on to them," he said of those who struggle with pornography, emphasizing the commonality of this sort of issue.

The faith leader said he occasionally comes across a person who recognizes that there are things within them that are "not of themselves," though he said those who recognize this need for deliverance on their own tend to be spiritually mature and are generally without a history of mental illness.

Deliverance ministry has become quite popular in modern Christian circles, though not everyone is on board with the practice.

Again, the terms surrounding spiritual warfare can get murky depending on how different people frame the associated issues. General deliverance itself obviously differs from exorcism in the ways we've discussed; interestingly, it has the tendency to make some Christians uncomfortable.

In a *Patheos* article published in 2017, Jack Wellman, pastor of the Mulvane Brethren Church in Mulvane, Kansas, tackled two key questions: Are deliverance ministries biblical, and are they taught in the Bible? Despite claims from those who have said they experienced relief as a result of deliverance ministry, Wellman took a different stance on these ministries.

Mirroring what others told me, Wellman noted in his piece that deliverance organizations "typically boast of the cleansing a person of demons or evil spirits in order to address problems manifested in their life as a result of the presence or possession of demons, who are said to be the root causes of their addictions, illnesses, or other problems."[28]

He went on to explain that the belief surrounding these paradigms is that demons can oppress and hold people in various sins and addictions, and that there are demons affiliated with drug, alcohol, or porn abuse, among other "demons of addiction," as some will call them. Wellman noted that deliverance is mentioned in the Bible more than 160 times—an impressive number of mentions in the text.

"It's a concept God obviously wants us to think about," he wrote. "God promised Abraham that He'd deliver him out of his enemy's hands (Genesis 14:20), God delivered Israel out of their Egyptian bondage (Exodus 18:8), and God delivered David out of all kinds of danger and fear (1 Samuel 17:35–37; Psalm 31:8)."[29]

And the references don't stop there, with the theme again emerging when Jesus was delivered over to be crucified. Wellman concluded that deliverance itself is a key term throughout the biblical arc, noting that "we are redeemed by the precious blood of the Lamb of God and delivered from the domain of darkness, so deliverance is a good thing."[30]

But while Wellman believes the Bible has much to say about deliverance, he differentiated the many scriptural mentions from what generally unfolds in deliverance ministry. Praying for people to overcome a sin is one thing, but laying hands on a Christian in an effort to get him or her to overcome a sin is an entirely different matter, he argued, and is "not biblical."

Wellman drove home his belief that a Christian cannot be possessed (a topic we'll address in the next chapter), though he argued that believers can certainly face spiritual attacks. Still, he believes no Christian who has the Holy Spirit would ever need any type of deliverance. So he rejects the idea that a Christian might need deliverance—something that some pastors and faith leaders would counter. Rather than deliverance ministry, Wellman believes Christians should focus on "telling people how they might be delivered from the wrath of God, which Jesus says abides on all who disbelieve."[31]

What do those practicing deliverance have to say? McEntire, who specializes in deliverance, responded to critics who might take a negative position on the spiritual practice and affirmed his experience dealing with these issues. "Some who claim that deliverance is unbiblical . . . do so to make a distinction between exorcism, which they believe to be biblical, and deliverance," he said. "Those who reject deliverance tend to find some of the issues identified by deliverance ministers to be unbiblical, such as generational bondage, being the target of a curse, or unhealed emotional wounds."

But McEntire said many of these critiques fly in the face of the experiences that he and many other ministers have personally confronted—events that these faith leaders affirm are both real and authentic. There's clearly a splintering between those who practice deliverance on Christians—people who see believers as being able to be afflicted by the demonic realm—and those who do not view deliverance as a relevant ministry among the faithful.

It's a fascinating dynamic with some fine theological lines that some are not willing to cross. A broader and more diabolical debate centers on whether a Christian can experience a full possession. While it's a prospect many Bible believers reject, it's yet another angle under the spiritual warfare umbrella that deserves due scrutiny and exploration.

11

POSSESSION OF CHRISTIANS?

I was trying to figure out how to kill myself." Amy Stamatis calmly uttered this proclamation as she shared with me the harrowing details of her tragic and traumatic journey—a story so intriguing that I felt compelled to track her down after learning some of the shocking details.

Stamatis was married with children and was working as a nurse at an Arkansas hospital in 2006 when something truly inexplicable happened: one night, she suddenly found herself confused and disconnected. Not long after, her behavior became erratic and she began to experience profound mental anguish. In the midst of what became a mountain of desperation and uncertainty, Stamatis's thoughts were consumed with ending her life—something she had never experienced before.

"I knew, being a nurse, if I shot myself I would maybe end up in a coma, and I wanted to do a good job," she recalled.

The dire situation culminated one day when Stamatis found herself sitting on a window ledge two and a half stories above a brick patio at her home. Though Stamatis doesn't recall all the details, she remembers feeling compelled to sit back in the windowsill, allowing herself to fall backward out of her home, through the air, and all the way to the ground. "It's a miracle that I'm alive, because I fell out of the window and I landed on that brick patio," Stamatis said. "It punctured both of my lungs. It broke my back in three places."

She had no broken arms or legs, indicating that she never even tried to break her fall—a remarkable detail that only adds mystery to her ordeal. The horrifying incident left Stamatis permanently paralyzed from the waist down—a daily reminder of what unfolded during this chaotic and unexplainable time in her life.

"My intention was to kill myself. I don't remember saying, 'Oh, I'm going to do it right now.' I just remember sitting in the window thinking, 'Yes, this would happen. This may kill me, this might do it,'" she told me. "Because I was so miserable."

Just seven months before the life-altering incident, Stamatis was living an entirely normal life, raising her family and working at the local hospital where she was eventually treated. A regular churchgoer, Stamatis described herself as a Christian before her affliction but said her faith wasn't deeply rooted. The problems specifically began one night while Stamatis was caring for a burn patient. In the midst of a typical hospital shift, something suddenly went terribly wrong.

"Right after I took care of him, I couldn't think, I was trying to do my chart, I couldn't even think to put my words down on my chart, and I ended up scribbling something down and then the ER was really, really busy," she told me. "And when the ER is busy . . . we're supposed to go help them out. And I went down to help them out and I . . . didn't even know what I was supposed to do."

Dazed and confused, Stamatis left the hospital and went home, but her situation only worsened. She was a marathon runner at the time and tried to go out for a jog with a friend, but rather than moving along the road, she found herself weaving all over the place.

Her abilities and focus were intensely impaired, and she was deeply concerned.

That's when Stamatis told her husband that she thought she was having a nervous breakdown, sparking a series of medical tests aimed at discovering what was really unfolding—but Stamatis said doctors didn't quite know what they were dealing with. At first, they assumed it was a mental affliction.

"They called the doctor and he gave me antidepressants, which [was] like giving me water . . . it did nothing, and I just escalated from there," she said. "And my husband ended up taking me to a psychiatric hospital." But problems with diagnosing the affliction persisted, and the psychiatrist felt it was physical and not mental, so Stamatis was sent for seizure testing back to the hospital where she once worked. That's when her circumstances became even more perplexing.

As friends came to visit, Stamatis reportedly told one of them that she "had a demon"—something she doesn't recall saying. Then came the true downward spiral, as Stamatis's behavior became increasingly erratic. It was all very perplexing to her friends and family, she said, considering she "never had any kind of psychiatric problems" beforehand.

"My oldest brother . . . when he came to see me, he said, 'Amy, I thought I knew what the term *crazy* meant and you put a whole different spin on it. I never, ever have seen anybody this crazy,'" she recounted.

This berserk behavior culminated in that life-shattering moment on her patio—a defining climax that horrified her loved ones and underlined the seriousness of her condition. Doctors and family members weren't sure at the time if Stamatis would survive, but as her church and community prayed, something fascinating happened.

A woman named Cindy Lawson—a stranger Stamatis had never met—heard about the story, prayed, and felt compelled to visit Stamatis in the hospital. Lawson believed Stamatis was being afflicted by demons, and later told KATV-TV about her experience in the hospital room. "The Lord spoke to me and told me to go to the hospital to cast the demons out of her. I could feel something churning," Lawson said, noting that she could tell something was wrong when she arrived in the room to pray. "I could see the demons."[1]

Stamatis purportedly spoke in an unfamiliar voice during the encounter, but that didn't dissuade Lawson, who prayed that the woman would be healed. "I looked at her, and a male voice came out of my mouth and said, 'What are you doing here?'" Stamatis recounted. "And I [later] told my husband that, and my husband started crying. He goes, 'Amy, you talked to me in that voice a couple of times.'"

Lawson reportedly prayed in Jesus' name during the hospital visit and demanded that any demons afflicting Stamatis be expelled. "She cast the demon out, and I do not remember that. I just remember she said, 'And I cast that demon out,'" Stamatis said. "My husband said he could tell something changed."

Stamatis said it took her some time after that transformational prayer to get back to normal, considering the amount of medicine she was on, but that she eventually cycled off all her medications and has not since experienced any mental afflictions. But the impact of the experience—and particularly the fall—has been long lasting.

"I'm paralyzed from my waist down," Stamatis told me. "It was such a struggle. I mean, this life is really hard to live. The house [we] live in, all the bedrooms are upstairs. So I ended up having a hospital bed in my living room, and we ended up having to convert our garage into a bedroom."

It took some time for Stamatis to fully comprehend all that had unfolded before she concluded without a doubt that she had been impacted by the demonic realm—and now she's hoping to help others who might find themselves facing the same battle. She decided to share her story with a local news outlet in October 2019, revealing the details of what unfolded—a decision that has had its own set of challenges, considering the strange reactions and skepticism that can often follow these stories.

But Stamatis is undissuaded, explaining that her goal is to show people that "there's freedom in Jesus." She specifically expressed a profound sadness for others in similar circumstances. "I would have either ended up locked up in a crazy house . . . or I would have been in prison," she said of her dire prospects had she not been healed. "And it makes me sad, because the people that are so oppressed like that, that's where they are. People don't know how to deal with it."

It's been more than a decade since Stamatis's life-changing fall. Today, her faith is deeper than it has ever been, and she's actively seeking to grow her relationship with Christ. "The enemy comes to steal, kill, and destroy," she said. "Jesus comes to give abundant life, and I'm seeking that abundant life."

A noteworthy element of Stamatis's story is her uncertainty on two key issues: the cause of her affliction and the nature of her faith walk before it all unfolded. A lot of people can point to experiences with sin or the occult as the basis of their problems with the demonic, but Stamatis said, "I don't know" when asked why she believes she was afflicted. "I was a Christian. I wasn't seeking God like I am now, but I didn't live bad; I was a good girl," she said. "I don't know. That's hard to say."

CHRISTIANS AND POSSESSION: INSIDE THE DEBATE

Stamatis's story poses a profoundly difficult theological question that was only hinted at in the previous chapter: Can a Christian become afflicted with a full possession (also known as an advanced deliverance)?

Dr. Shane Wood reframed the question in a truly thought-provoking way: "If you are saved, how can you be possessed by something that is damned—and does that affect my salvation?" Wood's presentation offers some additional elements that must be unpacked.

While it's true, in a biblical sense, that Christians face various degrees of oppression, the ability of a full spiritual takeover is an entirely different beast. Reverend Benjamin McEntire said that most of the people he works with through his deliverance ministry tend to be Christians who are experiencing spiritual affliction of some sort, but when it comes to oppression of non-Christians, he sees a pointed dynamic at play.

"I believe that if it's non-Christians, the enemy's approach is typically to do something to get them interested in the occult or keep them completely oblivious," he said, noting that entire books have been written on the topic of whether a Christian can be demonized.

McEntire said the conversation gets a bit murky, depending on how people choose to define the key terms. Catholics, for instance, might argue that a Christian could be possessed since possession is seen as control over the body of a person—something that "can happen independent of the will of the person."

"Now, when you start dealing with the Protestant definition, it always comes down to, 'No, Christians can't be possessed,'" he said. "Some . . . don't even have a framework for demonic oppression as a lower category of bondage, so [they conclude], 'No, a Christian can't have a demon because the presence of the Holy Spirit in the person keeps that from happening.'"

We see this dynamic at play with Pastor Jack Wellman's arguments on this topic, as the preacher kept his response to this question pretty clear in an opinion piece on the matter. He wrote, "Does a believer need deliverance? Can a Christian be bound by a demon? Nope."[2]

The pastor acknowledged that there is a spiritual war raging, but that Christians have already overcome the demonic realm through

Christ. "Yes, there's a spiritual war going on, and we're up against a powerfully potent, clever, invisible enemy . . . but we don't need some man's help to deliver us from our strongholds. . . . We need the strength of Christ," Wellman wrote. "Besides, 'everyone who has been born of God does not keep on sinning, but he who was born of God protects him, and the evil one does not touch him' (1 John 5:18 ESV)."[3]

Wellman's contentions are clear, but McEntire noted that the discussion has some finer points that require additional parsing. In his own ministry, McEntire doesn't use the terms *possession* and *oppression* to describe demonic bondage, proceeding to explain what the definitions to these words generally mean and how they are to be understood in practice.

"For me, oppression is typically an external activity of the enemy when they are weighing down on the person from the outside," he said. "Plus, it has the feeling of being oppressed, like a person's carrying a lot of heavy weight around."

As we've explored, possession (or advanced deliverance) is a scenario that is much more severe and internal in nature. Pastor Lucas Miles, who believes oppression can impact believers and nonbelievers alike, helped further illustrate the difference between how acts of oppression and possession might take form.

In the case of oppression, he said a person is still in full control of him- or herself—an important point that needs to be clarified for anyone looking to understand the theological complexities surrounding these issues. "When we accept Jesus as spirit into our life, he doesn't take over our life—we still have control over our life," he said. "I think the same way, when somebody is being oppressed by a spirit, they don't lose their free will totally. They still have the ability to have authority."

On a broader level, some theologians and pastors note that demonic oppression or influence takes form on a very wide spectrum. McEntire, for one, argued that the best term for any type of demonic bondage is "demonized" and explained that there is a wide range through which this dynamic can manifest.

"It exists on a spectrum," he said—one that can span from trivial or weak points of attachment that "exert almost no control over a person" and might translate into a mere annoying thought here or there to full-on possession, to a much more pervasive force.

Despite McEntire's belief that spiritual oppression can impact Christians, he said there are "certain degrees of bondage" that believers would not be able to experience. "They can still have some pretty severe demonization, and I've seen that before," McEntire said. "Yes, they're committed to Christ, but they still have very serious sin issues, past occult involvement, things like that, that have never fully been dealt with, if at all."

He continued, "So they may be coming to church, they do affirm Christ as Savior, but then there's all this other stuff that happens in their lives that many people don't know about, and then when they come for ministry, wanting help with those things, you find that there's a lot of demonic bondage. That is not uncommon."

Others like Reverend Samuel Rodriguez said they don't believe it's possible for a Christian to be possessed, though Rodriguez agreed that oppression, harassment, distraction, and other forms of spiritual warfare—experiences that would fall on the spectrum McEntire discussed—could certainly be experienced by the faithful.

Notably, though, he said the presence of the Holy Spirit inside of a Christian would preclude God's goodness and the enemy's evil from coexisting inside the same person. "Two objects cannot occupy the same space—simple law," Rodriguez said, referring to the inability of the Holy Spirit to coexist with the demonic inside of a believer.

Hank Hanegraaff mirrored this sentiment, contending that "if you're a believer, the kind of spiritual battle that you will be facing is different from the kind of battle that a nonbeliever would fight."

Hanegraaff pointed to Jesus' words in Luke 11:24–26 to fully explain this difference.

"Jesus points out that when an evil spirit comes out of a man, it goes through arid places, it seeks rest. It doesn't find it, and then it says, 'I'm going to return to the house that I once lived in,'" he said. "And when it arrives, it finds the house unoccupied, swept clean, and put in order. Then it goes and takes with it seven other spirits more wicked than itself and they go in and they live there and the final condition of that person is worse than the first."

Hanegraaff said the main takeaway is that a person who chooses to be "unoccupied by the Holy Spirit" subjects him- or herself to the possibility of being inhabited by the demonic, whereas those who have chosen to embrace Christ are in a different category.

"If our house is the house of Christ, the home of Christ, then the devil will find no place within that home," he added. "It is a radically different proposition for someone who is not indwelt by the Holy Spirit than for someone who is."

Dr. Michael Brown agreed with these assessments, but with some caveats. While he said he ultimately doesn't believe that "the Holy Spirit will dwell in the same place where Satan dwells" and that Christians' bodies "become temples of the Holy Spirit," the possibility for a believer to open the door to the demonic still remains.

"It may be semantics more than anything, because if someone has opened the door to the enemy and now come under the domination of the enemy, they need to be set free," he said. "Satan has taken ground in their lives and we need to drive Satan out of that ground so they can experience freedom again."

In the case of Christians, Brown wondered whether *possessed* is the right word to use, but posited that it is certainly possible for a Christian to "be demonized" and come under demonic power. Christians, he said, "can open doors like anyone else" and "believe lies like anyone else"—pathways and untruths that can be detrimental to believers' lives.

"They can play games with sin and with the dark realm like anybody else, and they can definitely get bound where they need to be set free," Brown said. "Now, in Jesus, we can't be bound unless we give ground, unless we open the door." So, if Christians give ground, it's possible, he believes, for a type of demonic infestation to take root—a scenario that could leave someone hindered or oppressed.

But Brown was careful to differentiate this sort of scenario from the total spiritual control we see depicted in most Hollywood films and in biblical accounts. While some people might end up "under the power" of a spirit as seen throughout the New Testament, Brown would argue that he doesn't see this form of full possession as a possibility for a believer.

There is a broader, timeless discussion about whether a Christian can lose his or her salvation, and this theological exploration certainly plays into views on demonic oppression. In a hypothetical situation in which a person opens a pathway to the demonic and loses his or her salvation, one could speculate that diabolical forms of influence on the upper end of the spectrum would suddenly become a possibility. That debate, though, won't be settled on these pages.

"If you walk back into the world, back into Satan's domain, you can be possessed and you can be harassed," Hanegraaff said, differentiating between the dynamics he believes unfold in "transactional Christianity" versus "transformational Christianity."

"In transactional Christianity, you say a prayer and now you receive a card that gets you into heaven and keeps you out of hell. Well, that's a transaction," he said. "In true Christianity, we're talking about transformation. And that transformation is progressive and it's very difficult."

Hanegraaff's point is that true Christianity requires an ongoing relationship and effort—and that leaves the possibility open, in his view, that someone could walk away from the faith or open him- or herself up to spiritual danger.

"The problem with much of modern-day Christianity is that it is transactional and not transformational," he said.

Regardless of whether a full possession can take form inside of a Christian, the main takeaway from many of the theologians and pastors interviewed for this book is that Christians are, at the least, at risk for spiritual attack.

Miles argues that Christians are in a sense "sealed," but that there are cracks and openings that can potentially take form depending on what is happening in a believer's life. "They're saved, they're redeemed, their spirit . . . is 100 percent, wall-to-wall Holy Spirit–infused at that point," he said of people who have embraced Christ.

But Miles pointed out that it's not uncommon to see some people who love Jesus struggling with intense depression and other issues that can, at times, have spiritual rooting. "All of us are susceptible to this, that we can be affected in our mental faculties, our mind, our will, and our emotions, by lies of the enemy," Miles said. "Which is one of the reasons why Paul tells us that we need to renew our minds, and that that's the work of the believer."

He continued, "My spirit's been redeemed, but I need to renew my mind in order to get it to look like what's in my spirit." As Miles detailed, this notion of renewing one's mind is seen in Scripture, with Paul writing the following in Romans 12:2: "Do not conform to the pattern of this world, but be transformed by the renewing of your mind. Then you will be able to test and approve what God's will is— his good, pleasing and perfect will."

For Christians, this verse is a reminder that God's will is discernible for any person who makes a concerted effort to decline to follow the world's lead and instead allow for the transformation and renewal of his or her mind. It's something Paul repeatedly drove home in his New Testament letters, with the theme again emerging in 2 Corinthians 4:16. He wrote that the body might be outwardly "wasting away" but that "inwardly we are being renewed day by day."

The idea here is that there is a responsibility for routine growth within a believer, with Paul further exploring these themes in Ephesians 4:20–24. Here, again, he called on Christians to be renewed in their lives, spirit, and minds:

> That, however, is not the way of life you learned when you heard about Christ and were taught in him in accordance with the truth that is in Jesus. You were taught, with regard to your former way of life, to put off your old self, which is being corrupted by its deceitful desires; to be made new in the attitude of your minds; and to put on the new self, created to be like God in true righteousness and holiness.

Miles said that Paul's advice for transforming our minds is essential to understanding this issue of spiritual oppression; he argued that becoming a Christian and then failing to pursue spiritual renewal will leave people vulnerable to negative forces in the spiritual realm.

"If somebody gets set free of a demonic oppression and they become a Christian, there's still an effort that might need to be made in renewing their mind," he said. "It might not automatically make them totally free of any symptoms of this sort of oppression. But it takes time for them to renew their mind in order to get these lies to be conformed into what the Word says about us."

During our interview on the subject, Wood returned to his original question about whether someone who is saved can be possessed "by something that is damned," arguing that it's possible that this inquiry is "simply beyond what we have biblical evidence to say."

The Bible scholar, like many of the others consulted for this book, said it's entirely possible to be close to Christ and still allow

Satan to impact our lives, appealing to the example of Judas Iscariot—one of the original twelve disciples who turned Jesus over to Jewish authorities. It's a shocking moment recounted in Scripture, with this ultimate betrayal of Christ leading to his crucifixion.

"You can be close to Jesus and still allow Satan to enter into you," Wood said. "Judas has to be the archetype for this; otherwise I don't know what happened with Judas. . . . Following Jesus, [he] was still able to allow Satan to completely enter him."

Wood pointed to the words in John 13, which tell us some intriguing details about Judas and Satan. We are told in this chapter that Jesus knew his time on earth was coming to a close. During an evening meal just before Passover, Christ washed his disciples' feet.

But before that pivotal moment, we're told something else in verse 2 that is pretty stunning: "The evening meal was in progress, and the devil had already prompted Judas, the son of Simon Iscariot, to betray Jesus." So, we know that Satan was, according to Scripture, clearly impacting Judas's decision making, and a bit later in the chapter we read something even more stirring and theologically disturbing about the disciple's spiritual condition.

After washing the disciples' feet, Christ predicted the betrayal that will soon befall him. "One of you is going to betray me," Jesus proclaimed (John 13:21). Christ then told the disciples that the person he was about to give a piece of bread to would be the man who would betray him. John 13:26–30 reads:

> Then, dipping the piece of bread, he gave it to Judas, the son of Simon Iscariot. As soon as Judas took the bread, *Satan entered into him.*
>
> So Jesus told him, "What you are about to do, do quickly." But no one at the meal understood why Jesus said this to him. Since Judas had charge of the money, some thought Jesus was telling him to buy what was needed for the festival, or to give something to

the poor. As soon as Judas had taken the bread, he went out. And it was night. (emphasis added)

"Satan entered into him." Those words are without a doubt tragic, troubling, and thought provoking, sparking a slew of questions about Judas, his heart, his salvation, and plenty more—questions that are perhaps impossible to answer two thousand years later. There are divergent theories surrounding where Judas's faith fell before this moment, why he turned so harshly against Jesus, and whether he could have been forgiven after his tragic betrayal of Christ.

Jesus made it clear that Judas—the man who was set to betray him—was in dire trouble. Christ said, "The Son of Man will go just as it is written about him. But woe to that man who betrays the Son of Man! It would be better for him if he had not been born" (Matthew 26:24).

And Jesus went even further, proclaiming, "Have I not chosen you, the Twelve? Yet one of you is a devil!" (John 6:70–71). The Bible makes it clear here that Christ was referencing Judas.

What's perhaps most interesting is that we see Judas realizing the full weight of his error, as he was suddenly "seized with remorse" after watching the chief priests and elders crafting their plans to kill Christ. He returned the thirty pieces of silver and recognized that he was gravely wrong—but it was too late.

"I have sinned," Judas said, "for I have betrayed innocent blood" (Matthew 27:4). After returning the silver, he hanged himself, placing the final touches on his own tragic ending while simultaneously leaving us all with a litany of questions. The debate about Judas's soul is a book within itself, but that's not our purpose here; the intention in referencing his story is to note that even someone with close physical proximity to Jesus—a person hearing and learning from Christ—could still be deeply influenced by Satan.

Remember: this was a man chosen by Christ to be an apostle.

He followed Jesus for more than three years, traveled around and sacrificed his own whims for the sake of Christ, personally viewed miracles, saw Jesus deliver the most timeless and powerful speeches and sermons imaginable, and was a witness for truth.[4] The fact that someone like Judas could "turn" is disturbing at best. The core of the issue is whether he was ever biblically saved and, thus, a Christian.

But the broader lesson is that any Christian holds the power to grant permission for evil to enter his life if he so chooses. "Christians can actually be Christians and still be granting permission for the unholy one to be a part of their lives," Wood said. "Now, what does that mean about their salvation? I do not know."

The Bible scholar argued that Judas is a prime example that "a follower of Jesus can actually be possessed by Satan." Still others take more definitive positions on Judas that would place him firmly in the camp of "never saved." For example, Matt Slick of the Christian Apologetics and Research Ministry believes that Judas was never a true Christian, so conversations about his faith journey—in Slick's view—are a bit easier to dismiss.

"Judas was never a true Christian," he wrote.[5] "Therefore, he never lost his salvation." Others agree with this assessment, with *Crosswalk* writing the following about Judas and the salvation debate:

> If someone asks, "Did Judas lose his salvation?" the answer is No. He didn't lose his salvation because he never had it. Whatever else you can say about him, he was never a follower of Jesus Christ in the same sense as the other apostles. He was not saved and then lost. He was lost because he was never saved in the first place.[6]

Again, Judas's life and death leave us with many questions. But if we cut through those questions, we are left with one reality that many of these faith experts agree with: anyone—Christians included—can summon or invite evil. And while there is a dispute surrounding the level to which spiritual oppression can take form in Christians' lives, it's clear that playing with fire can have deep and profound spiritual implications for any and all humans.

> *Playing with fire can have deep and profound spiritual implications for any and all humans.*

As for Stamatis, her case remains fascinating, and there are many others like her—people who believe their lives have been deeply impacted by the demonic realm. Regardless of what people believe about the potential impact of possession in a Christian's life, the Bible proclaims that spiritual warfare is certain to be experienced by all believers.

And if this experience and its potential pitfalls are universal, we must explore why so many churches choose to ignore or downplay this important biblical subject matter.

PART FIVE

THROUGH AN AUTHENTIC CHRISTIAN LENS

12

BREAKING DOWN THE
CHURCH'S SILENCE

There was a war in heaven. That war came down to earth. Adam and Eve lost that war. Jesus came—won that war."

Those words, passionately uttered by Pastor Mark Driscoll during a 2019 interview on *The Pure Flix Podcast*, got me thinking more deeply about spiritual warfare. This concept of a war in heaven and a spiritual battle that plays out on Earth are at the core of the Christian faith, yet how many of us truly understand these theological implications? How many of us process what it means in practice?

What Driscoll said next, though, further piqued my interest, curiosity, and wonder, as he framed this war narrative as having some definitive implications for each of our lives—parts of the puzzle we all need to piece together regardless of our whims.

"Now we have a choice to either walk into the defeat of Adam or walk in the victory of Jesus, and one day, Jesus comes back and there'll be one great war to end all wars, and so . . . the decisions you make, they're either inviting heaven down into your life or pulling hell up into your life," he said. "Because in the end there will only be two cultures: There will be the culture of heaven, [and] the culture of hell."

Aside from holding the power to convict us, these comments open up a discussion about good and evil that must be confronted. A basic reading of the Bible renders denying the existence of demons—at least from an authentic Christian lens—an impossibility.

As we have explored in this book, a great deal of Jesus' recorded ministry was spent dealing with spiritual healing, with the Christian Savior expelling spirits that overtook people's lives and caused intense evil; talk of angels in the Bible is also quite prevalent. "The Bible talks of angels more than three hundred times, and 90 percent of the books of the Bible speak about angels and demons," Driscoll said.

> *A basic reading of the Bible renders denying the existence of demons—at least from an authentic Christian lens—an impossibility.*

One could craft a theological argument to deny that demons today still have the same capabilities as we see in Scripture, though a blanket denial of their general existence seems strange for anyone who takes the Bible seriously—a point affirmed by pastor and *Good God* author Lucas Miles. "The Bible's very clear. If we believe in God, we have to therefore also believe in the devil and believe in demonic oppression and these things," Miles told me. "Because if the Bible is true and that's what we hold to, it acknowledges also that these things are real, and so we can't ignore them."

Dr. Michael Brown agreed, pointing to the Bible's blatant and intentional discussion about the existence and active nature of the spiritual realm. "The Bible speaks freely about demons and angels. The Bible tells us that we are in a battle with Satan himself," he said. "The Bible tells us that we're not wrestling with flesh and blood, but with demonic powers operating in a systematic, coordinated way. So to be sober-minded means to recognize the reality of the spiritual realm."

One of the dynamics at the core of this issue are the divergent ways different Christian denominations and movements handle the demonic. Some pastors and churches see these themes as having a great deal of prevalence and relevance in the modern era and address them as such, while others take a more reserved or apathetic stance. Certain churches might simply choose not to emphasize the existence of evil, opting to minimize or ignore it during sermons and official church teachings. The key question is why? What drives these differences, and how do they play out in practice?

Some preachers choose not to give attention to Satan and demons, believing that doing so gives undue credit to evil. For others, perhaps there's a fear of sorts that has taken root—a worry over the perceived strangeness of the subject matter at hand.

"I think sometimes it's a reticence to even talk about it because they feel maybe foolish or maybe there's fears—maybe the enemy has actually brought in fear," Grace Driscoll told me on *The Pure Flix Podcast*. "Since we don't know much about it or because the person, the school of thought, doesn't talk about it much, maybe they just feel fearful to even engage in that conversation."

Driscoll, who wrote the spiritual warfare book, *Win Your War: FIGHT in the Realm You Don't See for FREEDOM in the One You Do*, alongside her husband, Pastor Mark Driscoll, said it's important to show people that God has already won the war and that Christians have the power to fight back on a daily basis. "It's not that most Christian pastors or churches don't say anything," Pastor Mark Driscoll added. "They just say very, very little and they say it very quickly."

Chad Norris, senior pastor at Bridgeway Church in Greenville, South Carolina, speculated that fear over losing support for being too vocal on the issue might drive some of the silence. "Many of my fellow brothers and sisters that lead have such a strong fear of man," he said. "It's tied into money. They want to protect their jobs. I'm here. I don't care about that. I'm going to tell the truth—what I see biblically, what I've seen in real life."

Miles also pondered whether fear, worry, and discomfort might play a role in this scenario. "Many churches today . . . it seems to be a topic that they're afraid of going into," he said. "If they saw the stats, you would think that people would be wanting to talk about it, because the stats are showing that pop culture is picking this stuff up, so you would think it'd be safe to talk about in the church."

But Miles said speaking about themes surrounding the demonic feels like it could be "unpopular" or strange, which can lead to a slew of caveats in order to ensure that stories told about spiritual warfare are essentially buffered to be well-received by listeners. "If you tell a story about a spiritual warfare encounter, you have to insert all sorts of prefaces—'Well, I don't know for sure,' and 'This might not have been, but this is kind of what I think,'" he said.

Miles said this issue is not restricted only to discussions surrounding the demonic, as he sees people moving away from talking about the power of the Holy Spirit in the same manner. "There is a general hesitancy among [some] leaders in churches . . . we're afraid to talk about spiritual warfare, the power of the Spirit, something beyond just what can be reasoned with logic," he said. "We've become a very kind of Greek society in that way, where to some degree, it's a form of gnosticism, where we're worshiping what can be known. If it can't be known, we're not going to talk about it. We're not going to try to understand it."

Others see a reluctance or silence on the part of pastors and churches to be evidence of an even more pervasive theological issue: a move away from belief surrounding the demonic. "Why do I think the subjects of demons and spiritual warfare are given so little attention by some Christians?" Shane Idleman, founding pastor of Westside Christian Fellowship in Lancaster, California, rhetorically stated in an interview for this book, "Well, many people just don't believe they exist anymore, and they just kind of minimize it."

He continued, "But if you read the Bible, you clearly see that the demonic realm is real. Jesus cast them out; he took authority over them." At the same time, Idleman said, there's a dynamic on the opposite end of the spectrum that can sometimes present theological and practical issues: an over-emphasization or obsession with the demonic.

Some people, he said, see the demonic as the root of every single issue or problem, attributing all happenings to an evil, esoteric ream, a worldview that can lead to a lack of personal responsibility for issues that might befall us as a result of our own errors or mistakes. "We also should not give the demons too much credit. There's a lot of people that think there's a demon under every bush, or a demon attached to every problem, or a demon of this and that," Idleman said. "No, many times, you just need to humble yourself, and repent, and discipline the flesh. . . . So, be very careful there to find that balance."

Miles agreed, adding that there's no need to elevate elements in the demonic realm and that humans do not need to fear them either. Still, he said, "We can't ignore the presence of evil in this world if we believe in the presence of good."

Reverend Samuel Rodriguez summarized all of this by presenting his take on the "two streams of the church spectrum" that are actively unfolding today. First, he described a group he dubbed the "head Christian," or the person who acknowledges the reality of evil at a cerebral level.

"We have the cerebral cognitive church which says, 'I know evil exists, but much of the manifestations, much of the actions, or interactions, or reactions from certain elements of the Christian world, primarily the charismatic world, may be vastly exaggerated. Therefore we're going to keep this at the cerebral level,'" he said.

Rodriguez went on to break down a second stream of Christianity, which he dubbed the "heart Christian." These are believers who see evil for what it is, and who want to tackle it—and encourage other Christians to combat it—in their daily lives.

"[They believe] not only is evil real, evil must be confronted on a daily basis, and there are manifestations of evil and if we address it more people would be free," he said. "It's that group of people who actually believe that the purpose of the church is not just to preach the gospel and make disciples and fulfill the great commission, but to set people free from spiritual oppression."

Rodriguez continued, "That right there is a fundamental tenet of churches that want to address evil in a more measurable, viable, sustainable manner."

It might seem surprising, but there are times it seems as though Hollywood is covering the topic more intensely than some churches. And while Tinseltown isn't always biblically accurate when it presents possession and other spiritual issues, the attention that movies and TV have paid to these themes is noteworthy. "With the exception of probably some stronger charismatic churches that I'm aware of, I would say that I think Hollywood and pop culture probably talk more about the faith side of spiritual warfare and the demonic more so than the church a lot of times," Miles said.

The pastor—who is also a film producer—did not argue that Hollywood is accurately depicting these issues but spoke to the fact that certain films and shows are presenting story lines about spiritual battles or clashes between good and evil. And these themes, which have long been a Hollywood horror staple, seem to be ticking up in popularity.

In real life, though, the struggle for balance is intriguing. Some simply believe that the "demon behind every door" narrative is being counterbalanced with a "we can only embrace the here and now" mindset. "It seems like the pendulum has moved to the other side of the spectrum, and we're now at a point to where this has really taken a back seat in Christian communication and language," Miles said.

Brown emphasized this same point, adding his belief that we tend to "swing to extremes." When people "blame the devil for everything," he argued that they tend to miss the mark on things that happen through natural causes. He added that it's often "easy to just look in the natural and look at earthly things and have earthly explanations for them."

And when we consider the fast pace at which our lives and culture are moving—and the constant distractions we have that keep us consumed and enamored by the material—it makes sense why some of us might be overly fixated on the here and now. Smartphones and tablets have all but overtaken our attention and daily downtimes, with media messages increasingly hitting us when we are at home or on the go.

With so much of the material world before us, it is no wonder why so many of us have lost our sense of biblical reality, especially if we are not making it a priority to create and foster an active spiritual life. That's likely where much of the problem starts. "Sometimes, it's a lack of being spiritually minded," Brown confirmed. "It's a lot easier for me in the natural to just look at earthly things and look at political trends and look at social trends and look at what's happening in my own family without recognizing that often there are spiritual forces behind this. And Scripture speaks to this plane." He added, "This is really not a debatable issue for a Bible believer."

Rodriguez, who described himself as an evangelical Christian who is "Bapticostal," warned that it is too easy nowadays to become apathetic to the spiritual realm, adding his belief that there's a "bougie Christianity" afoot.

"I know evil exists. I've confronted it. I know what spiritual warfare is on steroids. I lived it," he said. "Sometimes it becomes so cerebral—and I call it 'bougie Christianity'—we become so bougie . . .

we become so sophisticated in our thinking and we lose the fact, the sense that there is spiritual warfare, there is darkness."

Rodriguez pointed to John 10:10 in the Bible as a verse that he believes perfectly captures "the reality of spiritual warfare" and the "reality of our collective existence." That scripture reads: "The thief comes only to steal and kill and destroy; I have come that they may have life, and have it to the full." The pastor called the dynamic described in this Bible verse as the "great dichotomy," addressing Jesus' words pointing to him (Christ) as the solution.

"Here's the devil; here's who I am. And this guy over here comes to rob, kill, and destroy," Rodriguez said. "Every single day, there's an attempt to rob, kill, and destroy."

Spiritual warfare manifests itself in a variety of ways in people's lives, with pastors and theologians explaining the impact they have personally observed. We've covered both the biblical stories and modern-day claims, and what's most interesting is that these experiences share similarities with manifestations of mental illness.

Next, let's explore the debate over possession and mental illness—and how pastors, theologians, and mental health experts differentiate.

Now, let's explore what it purportedly looks like when the devil acts out on these plans.

13

POSSESSION VERSUS ILLNESS

Objects flying off of shelves. Personal details spewing out of a stranger's mouth that no one could have possibly known. And diabolical voices manifesting out of thin air.

These were just some of the shocking happenings that psychiatrist Dr. Richard Gallagher encountered when he met a woman he refers to as Julia, a self-described devil worshipper who simultaneously revered Satan while also seeking to be freed from the grips of the demonic forces that purportedly came along with her infatuation.[1]

Gallagher, a respected psychiatrist who studied medicine at Yale and Columbia and now teaches at both Columbia and New York Medical College, was transformed by his experience with Julia, as he recounted in an interview with CNN[2] and detailed in a fascinating *Washington Post* op-ed.[3]

"In the late 1980s, I was introduced to a self-styled Satanic high priestess. She called herself a witch and dressed the part, with flowing dark clothes and black eye shadow around to her temples," Gallagher explained. "In our many discussions, she acknowledged worshipping Satan as his 'queen.'"[4]

Gallagher, who prides himself on being a man of science, was initially approached by a Catholic priest to see if he could step in to assess whether Julia was suffering from some sort of mental ailment—or whether she was truly experiencing the demonic. At first, Gallagher wrote that he was "inclined to skepticism," but he soon recognized that Julia's behavior went above and beyond what he had experienced in his professional training.

From speaking languages she purportedly didn't know during her trances, such as Latin, to an ability to reveal a person's "secret weaknesses" to having private information on the deaths of people she had never known (including Gallagher's own mother), there was no shortage of strange elements surrounding Julia's case.[5]

But the most shocking and undoubtedly creepiest moment came when Gallagher said he and Julia's priest were talking on the phone one day. Julia wasn't on the call and was thousands of miles away at the time of the conversation, but Gallagher and the priest purportedly simultaneously heard one of the voices that had manifested from Julia during her demonic trances.[6]

"This was not psychosis; it was what I can only describe as paranormal ability," Gallagher wrote. "I concluded that she was possessed."[7] Unfortunately, Julia was never healed of her affliction, as Gallagher said she was torn and seemed to enjoy some of what unfolded during her alleged trances; as time progressed, she reportedly stopped seeking help from Gallagher.

But while her healing failed, it was the start of Gallagher's foray into combatting the demonic. It catapulted Gallagher, a lifelong Catholic, on an unlikely path to becoming a consultant of sorts for the Catholic Church, entering into cases like Julia's to offer scientific explanations while also pinpointing the rare instances he believes people are experiencing a so-called full possession.

Gallagher has been on this journey for twenty-five years now and believes that he has likely "seen more cases of possession than any other physician in the world"—a notable claim that places him in a truly unique position.[8]

After consulting on hundreds of cases, he now openly discusses his work, sharing details about his initial skepticism, his evidence-based approach to the demonic, and how he remedies being a staunch practitioner of science who simultaneously believes that diabolical manifestations of the supernatural are possible, plausible, and, in some cases, an undisputed reality.

His role as a doctor isn't necessarily to diagnose possession, but as he noted in his *Washington Post* op-ed, he aims to "inform the clergy that the symptoms in question have no conceivable medical cause."[9] What's perhaps most interesting about Gallagher is his careful approach. He is fully aware of the oftentimes ill-conceived and dangerous religious handling of demonic claims—one that can lend itself to overdiagnosis of demonic influence within some church circles.

But he's also not afraid to speak out about his belief that some in the medical field err in their refusal to look at evidence for the supernatural. In the end, Gallagher believes it all comes down to facts, evidence, and due diligence. "The same habits that shape what I do as a professor and psychiatrist—open-mindedness, respect for evidence and compassion for suffering people—led me to aid in the work of discerning attacks by what I believe are evil spirits and, just as critically, differentiating these extremely rare events from medical conditions," he wrote.[10]

And Gallagher said he's not alone. While some tend to see psychologists, psychiatrists, and other medical professionals as siloed in the world of science that only sees answers to our life and world through a material lens, he knows other mental health practitioners who are open to his conclusions.

Gallagher also isn't the first doctor to speak out on this topic, as the late Dr. M. Scott Peck also found himself diving so deep into the foray that he personally participated in two exorcisms—experiences he revealed through his writings. These stories were covered in detail by the *Los Angeles Times*, with the outlet writing the following in a 1985 story:

> The psychiatrist is firm in his insistence that he encountered Satan. He described one possessed patient as actually becoming serpentine in appearance, with hooded eyelids, and the other as becoming so grotesque and inhuman that Peck, when he tried later in front of a mirror, was unable to contort his face into such a diabolic grimace.[11]

Peck, another Harvard-educated professional, also detailed these experiences in his final book, *Glimpses of the Devil: A Psychiatrist's Personal Accounts of Possession*, with the book's description touting itself as offering "the amazing true story of his work as an exorcist . . . in two profoundly human stories of satanic possession."[12]

What's most compelling about Peck is that he purportedly didn't believe in Satan—until he met one of the subjects involved in these exorcisms. He even assumed that the case might help affirm the contention that belief in the devil was unwarranted.

But he was wrong, as the description notes that "what he discovered could not be explained away simply as madness or by any standard clinical diagnosis."[13] And, affirming just how pivotal these cases were, he told *Salon* the following in a 2005 interview: "The evidence I found defied my belief and I ended up being converted."[14]

These exorcisms involved teams comprised of medical professionals and religious leaders, with the first including a nun, bishop, housewife, psychologist, retired doctor, and layman, and the second including two psychologists, two psychiatrists, three laypeople, and a minister, as the *Times* noted.[15] And both exorcisms took months, with time elapsing between looking at diagnoses of possession and moving forward with the actual exorcisms.[16] The first lasted a total of seven months and the second went on for nine months.

"In the first case, we got rid of four different demons, each representing a particular lie. After getting rid of these four, there only seemed to be two left, the demons of lust and hate," Peck told the outlet. "Those two were surprises to the team. The demons spoke in the third person. Whether that reflects something about demons' reality, I don't know, but it hid behind Jesus."[17]

The juxtaposition surrounding the two cases is quite fascinating, as the first involved a young woman Peck called Jersey. She said she had been afflicted by demons for fifteen years, but the account of her exorcism—as recounted in *Glimpses of the Devil*—was relatively benign.[18]

Salon described it as "a sedate and civilized affair, almost disappointingly free of the kind of bile-spitting, levitating, teeth-gnashing we know from movies like William Friedkin's *The Exorcist*," again pointing to what many experts have said: that exorcisms aren't always the horror show people assume.[19]

Jersey's exorcism was a success, but the second patient—known as Beccah—wasn't so fortunate. Plus, her exorcism experience was a bit more chaotic. Severely depressed and suicidal, she tried to bite Peck and the team, had to be restrained, and even put her hand through a bathroom window, as *Salon* recapped.[20] Tragically, she was not relieved of the purported demonic infestation and later died.

> *Exorcisms aren't always the horror show people assume.*

The key takeaway when exploring the work of Peck and Gallagher is that these men—well-known and respected psychiatrists—took professional risks to come forward with these claims. Many have and certainly will doubt their purported experiences, but it's essential to consider the noteworthiness of their stature and their willingness to openly address the complexities surrounding mental health and spiritual oppression.

It's also important to note that their experience involves more extreme examples of spiritual warfare, as many experts consulted for this book noted that full possession is incredibly rare. Gallagher himself has said that he spends "more time convincing people that they're not possessed than they are."[21]

But it's also essential to note that Gallagher and Peck are not alone in their claims. Dr. Mark Albanese, a psychiatrist for decades who was educated at Cornell University and is friends with Gallagher, has openly defended the psychiatrist. Albanese told CNN that he believes there is an increasing belief among doctors that humans' spiritual dimension must be considered regardless of a doctor's personal stance on the matter.

"There's a certain openness to experiences that are happening that are beyond what we can explain by MRI scans, neurobiology or even psychological theories," he told the outlet.[22]

A broader conversation about the intersection of demonic influence and mental affliction is surely warranted, especially considering that many of the symptoms attributed to spiritual issues seem to mirror those documented among people suffering from mental health struggles.

ONE PSYCHIATRIC NURSE'S JOURNEY TO FAITH

Dr. Mary D. Moller has been a psychiatric nurse for almost forty years and in 1992 founded the nation's first independent, nurse-managed, owned, and operated psychiatric clinic. She has a captivating perspective on mental health and the demonic realm; she believes there are essential pieces of the human puzzle that must be fully assembled to properly understand what's unfolding inside of a person.

"I believe that man is body, mind, and spirit. And so our brain, which is part of our body . . . can have glitches and people can have mental illness," Moller told me. "This is well documented. That's not an issue." But she wasn't done there. Going on to address the spiritual realm, Moller continued, "And I truly believe that our spirit is breathed into us from God and that the spiritual life is what God wants us to have and it's going to be in conflict with what our body wants and what our brain often wants."

Moller, an expert on treating schizophrenia, has openly shared her journey to Christianity—one that emerged as a result of an in-depth exploration of the intersections between faith and psychiatry. She revealed much of this experience in a 2014 article in the academic journal titled *Narrative Inquiry in Bioethics*, noting that she saw many patients who were victims of "severe and often brutal trauma" at the hands of family, spiritual leaders, friends, and others.[23]

Another area from which she has seen patients suffer? The occult. "We also uncovered sources of abuse suffered from those involved in occult practices ranging from seemingly innocent white witchcraft (Wicca, Paganism, New Age) that includes such activities as astral projection and remote viewing to the darkest possible black witchcraft (perpetrating evil, incanting evil spirits, casting spells and hexes, creating dissociative identities) such as occurs in ritual abuse and satanic rites," she wrote.[24]

Moller was cognizant of the fact that there is "controversy surrounding the reality of witchcraft," but noted that she wanted to share her story in an effort to help "break down the barriers that prevent many patients from receiving the treatment that would provide the most benefit to recovery." And that journey led to stunning transformation not only for Moller but for her patients as well. It was in seeking services for individuals impacted by these phenomena that she said she experienced a "Christian born-again experience" at fifty years old—a transformation that changed her life.

It was a conversion that took root in the winter of 1997 when Moller met a patient from a local mission—a man who was believed to have been involved with a satanic cult.[25] Moller, who had no experience with these sorts of issues at the time, didn't give it much thought until she encountered another patient in March of that year.

This woman, who was being evaluated for schizophrenia and had traveled a long way from Portland, Oregon, to meet Moller, had been hospitalized a number of times, but treatment wasn't working. So Moller sat down with the young women to hear her story. "I said to her, 'Has something awful happened to you?' And . . . just the floodgates opened," Moller told me of her experience. "She just started sobbing and I thought, 'Oh my gosh, what do we have going on here?'"

And what the girl said next absolutely shocked Moller to her core. "Through the course of the interview I learned she had been a victim of repeated satanic ritual abuse at the hands of her father, the head warlock of a coven," the nurse later wrote of the experience. "At least ten times she reported she had been ritually impregnated and then ritually aborted to provide a live fetus for human sacrifice rituals."[26]

The story sounds like something ripped from a Hollywood horror film (Moller herself echoed this when she shared other purported details too horrific to account here and said, "That's not even been in movies"). But despite the almost unbelievable nature of the story, Moller believed the woman.

The nurse told the family to report the case to local police. Years later, she said officers she met from the area confirmed that the story was true and that the woman's father was imprisoned. The story and its stunning aftermath was the start of a journey that led Moller to look beyond the realms of the physical and mental to explore how faith can also be integrated to help treat patients. It was her own personal journey that uncovered what she believes is definitive evidence that demons and spiritual warfare are real.

Eventually, she started integrating prayer and faith into her practice, but she hit some roadblocks along the way. As she began to learn more about the spiritual realm, Moller attempted to speak with some Catholic priests, but was repeatedly told, "You don't know what you're messing with."

The nurse felt brushed aside. After all, Moller was well aware that some patients were experiencing phenomena she had never dealt with—but she wanted answers, not only about the causal factors but about how she could help usher in healing. "I started going to training to learn about deliverance and psychiatry and demonism and who was really a solid teacher, [and] who wasn't," Moller told me. Over time, she learned more about deliverance, and her faith and started encountering additional patients who needed help.

The end result was a robust and successful effort to help those in need. "My professional career grew in nearly indescribable terms as a result of the incorporation of prayer and deliverance ministry as part of the services we selectively provided," she wrote.[27] "Today I always include assessment of spiritual experiences a patient has as well as spiritual supports that are available with every new patient intake."

Moller emphasized the importance of carefully approaching these issues and "distinguishing between religious experiences and religious delusions," and also stressed the need for mental health professionals to understand the beliefs of patients and not to judge based on personal biases.

A denial of the existence of these issues can, at times, harm recovery, she added. "Once I witnessed the level of healing that occurs with carefully administered spiritual interventions that are related to specific spiritual experiences that are based on the patient's belief system, there was no going back to using only allopathic medication and non-spiritual psychosocial interventions, even in spite of the criticisms from others," Moller wrote.[28]

The nurse's experience is a notable one, especially as we navigate realms in which some medical professionals dismiss claims such as hers.

BALANCING MENTAL HEALTH AND DEMONIC AFFLICTION

The discussion about demons, spiritual warfare, and mental health can sometimes be undoubtedly complex, especially in our materialistic era. One element that cannot be ignored is the oftentimes legitimate fear that mismanagement of mental health, lack of experience dealing with these matters, and over-spiritualization of nearly every scenario can lead to dangerous situations.

When someone believes there's a "demon behind every doorway," he or she could be prone to making improper assumptions about causal factors—assumptions that overlook the pitfalls of personal responsibility and errors and the effects of mental illness. From tragic attempts to beat demons out of the afflicted to other questionable actions aimed at expelling evil, some ill-conceived "remedies" have risked people's safety and lives. Critics point to these tactics when exploring the potential negative impact of possessions and spiritual healings.

And it doesn't take much effort to uncover some of the most disturbing examples, as a simple Internet search exposes what unfolds when attempts to expel purported evil go terribly wrong.

There's the case of an Arizona man accused of drowning his six-year-old son by placing the boy's face under streaming hot water in an effort to remove what he purportedly believed to be a demon.[29] Then there's the case of twenty-five-year-old Vilma Trujillo, a Nicaraguan woman who died after attempts to expel what a local pastor apparently believed to be a demon.[30]

Trujillo started hallucinating, talking to herself, and experiencing signs some would attribute to mental illness. When a local church in her remote town stepped in, she was reportedly "held captive," not given food or water, tied to a tree, and burned alive. The belief was that the fire would expel evil; the end result, though, was Trujillo's horrific death—a fatal error that shocked her nation.[31]

We could spend a plethora of time looking at other examples, though there is no need. The key takeaway is that bad theology and misplaced "solutions" to perceived spiritual problems can wreak damaging or deadly havoc. This is why any legitimate expert on the topic will devote significant effort toward understanding the mental states of individuals believed—or even suspected to be—facing oppression, possession, or demonic influence.

"Spiritual warfare can affect someone mentally, but there are also mental maladies that ought to be treated as such," Hank Hanegraaff told me. "Which is to say that if you have a mental malady and you are treating it in the wrong way or not treating it at all and relegating this only to spiritual warfare . . . just to use the medical analogy, we would call that malpractice."

It's implicit that this sort of due diligence is found in the work of people like Gallagher and Peck—and it can also be seen among faith leaders who are often the first in the field to hear from people feeling the weight of spiritual affliction. Before diving into an exorcism or deliverance, these experts generally attempt to understand every element of a patient's case.

"You have to be very careful if you're a priest or a pastor not to engage in malpractice. These days you need to be very careful as a doctor not to engage in malpractice," Hanegraaff said. "So, if there are psychophysical problems, then you have to seek a psychophysical solution to those problems."

How Christians Differentiate Between Mental and Spiritual

It's noteworthy that one area of commonality between Protestant and Catholic leaders is the quest to investigate whether a person is experiencing mental afflictions rather than spiritual manifestations—with an emphasis being placed on evaluating a person to explore psychological, psychiatric, and medical considerations before entering into exorcisms.[32]

The *Catechism of the Catholic Church*, which details Catholic belief and theology, addresses exorcism and describes the process as one that unfolds "when the Church asks publicly and authoritatively in the name of Jesus Christ that a person or object be protected against the power of the Evil One and withdrawn from his dominion."[33]

While the catechism goes on to briefly describe what it means to expel evil, it differentiates between spiritual and mental matters. "Illness, especially psychological illness, is a very different matter; treating this is the concern of medical science," the document reads. "Therefore, before an exorcism is performed, it is important to ascertain that one is dealing with the presence of the Evil One, and not an illness."[34]

It's clear that most Protestants and Catholics make a concerted effort to engage in solid, evidence-based exploration to understand exactly what's unfolding on both spiritual and mental planes.

As we've explored throughout the text of *Playing with Fire*, most experts clearly agree that full possession is very rare—and Reverend Benjamin McEntire, an Anglican priest who deals with the demonic, is no exception. "If I get somebody that I don't know [and] they come to me and say, 'I'm possessed' or 'I have lots of demons attached to me,' my immediate response to that is to be very skeptical," he told me. "At least in this society, the enemy mostly focuses on trying to hide, which is why if a person believes their problem to be demonic, there is a very high degree of probability it isn't and it's actually mental health issues."

Considering that the symptoms of spiritual and mental affliction seem to mirror each other, it's worth exploring the most common symptoms people purportedly suffering from demonic affliction claim to experience. McEntire has seen some commonalities in various cases surrounding spiritual affliction, though he can't say for sure that these same symptoms would emerge in every case.

"Normally, intrusive thoughts or feelings tend to factor in," he said. "So, that can be anywhere from that you're hearing voices in your mind to just certain types of thoughts come into their mind at particular times or about specific issues." Additionally, he said there are certain types of emotional impulses that can unfold, including compulsive behaviors.

On the surface, these seem like elements one could certainly attribute to mental affliction, so when asked more specifically to explain how he differentiates, McEntire obliged. "Demons react to certain types of commands, and mental illness won't," he said, noting that a demonic force will stop speaking voices and chaos into someone's mind if a qualified minister demands that the spirit stop doing so.

But he said it's a different dynamic when it comes to voices and chaos that result from mental affliction. "Mental illness simply doesn't respond to any form of exorcism and deliverance. A person can have demonic issues and not have mental health issues," he said. "I found it is fairly rare for a person to have mental health issues and not have some kind of demonic interference with it. To me, that just makes sense. Why would they not interfere with that?"

Moller also told me that she has learned through her work how to differentiate between mental illness and spiritual affliction, mirroring McEntire's experience. "I know mental illness and I know that when someone is describing things to me and they're not giving me a trajectory, that's mental illness," she said. "They're very lucid, know what they're talking about, and I listen and I see in their eyes that there's something else."

Dr. Mohab Hanna, a child and adolescent psychiatrist from New Jersey, also addressed the complexities of the human heart and mind in an interview for this book, agreeing with Moller's perspective on our mental, physical, and spiritual components. Hanna contended that we are all physical beings who have a "spiritual component to us." The interaction between the material and spiritual can create scenarios in which a psychiatric condition can "make somebody vulnerable to spiritual attack." "When people are anxious, or depressed, or they're psychotic, their view is skewed," Hanna said. "It's not accurate."

The level of emotional distress, he said, can distort one's ability to recognize and process truth—and he believes that's a reality that must be confronted and understood. "When people are really anxious—and I obviously see people with some pretty severe stuff, or severe depression, or suicidality . . . it's so distressing that it's so hard for them to see the truth of God's goodness," he said.

Pastor Mark Driscoll pointed to the fact that human beings have a "physical body and the immaterial soul" and expressed his own belief that these components affect each other. "If you're dealing with chronic pain and illness and lack of sleep, your spiritual state is affected," he told *The Pure Flix Podcast*. "Similarly, everything could be going well in your life, but things could be going poorly in your soul. And so these two realms, they are typified even in our existence, and they impinge upon one another."[35]

Hanna shared the example of a patient who had real psychiatric symptoms, but who also experienced a tremendous amount of doubt about her faith and Jesus' love. He said this mixture of the mental and spiritual shows an important area of overlap in which one component flows into the other. "When Christians are struggling in this manner, psychiatrically in my mind, it does cross the line into where I genuinely believe there's a spiritual component going on that they're very core faith is being attacked," Hanna said.

Some Christians might also experience anxiety over their past sins, face repeated reminders of their errors, and wonder whether Jesus can truly forgive them for what they've done—a direct assault on the basic elements of their faith: salvation and worthiness of forgiveness, he said.

"It's not uncommon for Christians, specifically . . . where . . . what is being questioned is the basis of their faith," Hanna said. "I find kind of remarkable that I've seen this repeatedly in Christians . . . where what is being attacked is the most fundamental part of their belief system."

While some mental health professionals and pastors experience seeing some of the more diabolical examples described by Gallagher and others, Hanna said his work led him to observe more subtle—albeit diabolical—spiritual attacks on the core of believers. "My experience has been not the dramatic, but I think just as distressing is the vulnerability where you're struggling with depression [and] there's a direct attack on your whole identity in Christ, whether you're loved or not, whether Jesus forgives a certain sin," he said. "To me, that's a pretty heinous attack, and think of the amount of distress this generates."

Hanna continued, "So that's where I see that when people are struggling psychiatrically, they are vulnerable to spiritual attack, and on Christ's identity and their identity in Christ." In these circumstances, Hanna said it all comes down to "truth" and helping patients see through the fog of their internal chaos to recapture the reality of the basis of their faith.

He helps these patients realize that "anxiety and depression put a lot of thoughts into your mind, and Satan can run with those." Hanna argued that the devil will make people believe various lies and that it's important to help Christians struggling in this regard look back to their ultimate authority: God and the Bible. "You try to help people to realize, 'What is truth?'"

His mention of these more subtle afflictions is an important component of this discussion, as much of the focus on the demonic is on the Hollywood-esque fanfare we see in movie portrayals of possessions and incidents of oppression.

But what if there's a more sinister and subtle form of spiritual suffering that causes us to question the basis of belief—what if there's a slow moving, under-the-radar catalyst for spiritual chaos that can seep into our hearts and minds and harm us in our weakest moments? "We're always looking for the big stuff, and the dramatic stuff, and the stuff that gets everybody's attention," Hanna said. "But I think, 'What about the daily stuff that when people experience, even with physical illness, when someone's in pain, they're vulnerable?'"

This mention of the dangers of the "subtle" influence of the demonic is thought provoking, and it's something other experts have explored. Albanese, who defended Gallagher's belief in the demonic in a 2008 letter to the editor in the Catholic magazine *New Oxford Review*, affirmed that possession is rare—but offered some thoughts along this same wavelength.

"As Dr. Gallagher states, possession is very rare. Much more common is subtle satanic influence. If you miss the subtlety, it can be at times obvious," Albanese wrote. "I am writing this letter on Good Friday. This very day, in a nearby town, several Christian churches were vandalized with spray-painted satanic symbols. I doubt that the timing was coincidental."[36]

If these subtle and not-so-subtle influences are indeed legitimately caused by the demonic realm, there are ramifications for both the individual and our culture at large. There are times Hanna might recommend pastoral counseling rather than misattributing various issues to mental affliction. The differentiation comes from investigating the issues at play in an effort to help people process through the problems they face and the root causes of their distress.

"We're spiritual beings, and as we go through life every single day and every decision we make, every thought we get, there's a spiritual component to it," Hanna said. "I genuinely believe there are demons, but, I think psychiatric illness by its nature just opens up people to so much spiritual attack on the most basic fundamental things of who they are as a human being created in God's image and who Jesus is."

Reading through the lines of Hanna's perspective, it's easy to see how one could argue that a psychiatric illness could open the door to oppression, but he was careful to also note that oppression "could look like a mental illness." That's why he's among those who argue that "an astute clinician or a pastor" should be involved to help decipher between the two.

It's worth mentioning an important point made by Driscoll, who noted that the books of Luke and Acts—New Testament texts that address possession and the supernatural—were written by Luke, a physician who is also an essential Christian figure.[37] Considering Luke's dual role and the multipurpose roles of people like Gallagher, Peck, and Moller, Driscoll made a thought-provoking point about the intersection of the mental and spiritual.

"I think the best way to minister to a person is to minister to the whole person. If all you do is treat the physical symptoms and maybe not some of the causation that's spiritual, you're not going to see the kind of healing and health that people could endure and enjoy," he said. "If all you do is just spiritualize everything and tell them, 'You don't need to take medication. You don't need to go to the doctor,' I think then we're neglecting the body."

This book won't settle the debate over our mental and spiritual components, but, at the least, the leaders and mental health practitioners covered in this chapter leave us with a great deal to ponder as we consider the ways in which these complexities play out in the real world.

14

Spiritual Impact on Our Culture

"If I had to pick one word to explain our culture today, I would use the word *war*."[1]

Pastor Mark Driscoll's simple summation of our current state of affairs caused me to pensively pause and consider the weight of his proclamation.

War.

That's a weighty and provocative word, yet it's perhaps the perfect way to frame the current state of idiosyncratic, chaotic, and morally relativistic affairs that are continuing to ramp up in our society. Why are we wading into such a profoundly confounding moral vacuum? How in the world did we get here?

Human history is without a doubt fraught with chaos, division, deadly decisions, and immensely damaging error, so immorality and ethical meandering are nothing new. The Scriptures themselves expose countless stories about diabolical human antics, and troubling and consequential behaviors that were already raging (and even normative) thousands of years ago.

Still, there does seem to be something different, transcendently sweeping and oddly uniform, happening in our culture today, with the Internet and technology connecting people as never before and perpetuating ideas and twisted norms across geographic boundaries.

When we see the many fronts of cultural "war" that Driscoll described playing out before us, we are faced with deeper questions about what is driving our cultural and ideological change and how we are intended to navigate through these evolutions to maintain a biblical worldview. There's also the unexpected element of wondering what happens next.

Most of this book has dealt with individual issues pertaining to claims of spiritual warfare, but it goes without saying that our individual journeys and experiences coalesce to comprise our collective whole. Plus, any serious Christian is bound to at least pay mind to the fact that the Bible itself claims to offer up prophetic words about what society will look like as humanity marches toward the biblical end of days and, ultimately, Christ's return.

Secularists, atheists, and agnostics are among those who no doubt dismiss the belief that Jesus will one day return or that people writing biblical texts thousands of years ago somehow had prophetic knowledge from God about future events that would unfold millennia past their deaths. Regardless of skepticism surrounding prophecy, one cannot deny that revelation and end-times theology are central components to biblical understanding.

We won't go deep into the end-times discussion here, though it's worth mentioning as it pertains to this subject of spiritual warfare. There is a great deal of scriptural content on the topic and much of it is debated, but Matthew 24 records Jesus' disciples asking for signs of his second coming and the end of days. Christ's answer is quite fascinating:

Watch out that no one deceives you. For many will come in my name, claiming, "I am the Messiah," and will deceive many. You will hear of wars and rumors of wars, but see to it that you are not alarmed. Such things must happen, but the end is still to come. Nation will rise against nation, and kingdom against kingdom. There will be famines and earthquakes in various places. All these are the beginning of birth pains.

Then you will be handed over to be persecuted and put to death, and you will be hated by all nations because of me. At that time many will turn away from the faith and will betray and hate each other, and many false prophets will appear and deceive many people. Because of the increase of wickedness, the love of most will grow cold, but the one who stands firm to the end will be saved. And this gospel of the kingdom will be preached in the whole world as a testimony to all nations, and then the end will come. (vv. 4–14)

There's a lot to further explore here, and I dealt with the over-arching end-times debate in my book, *The Armageddon Code: One Journalist's Quest for End-Times Answers*. But one of the central beliefs many Christians embrace is that society is marching toward even more chaos, with a great number of prophetic events set to take place around Israel and the Middle East (when you consider that Israel didn't re-emerge until 1948, these writings become even more fascinating).

Jesus' words in Matthew point to some of this individual and societal disorder that will be said to unfold during the end times. After reading the passage, it's hard to deny that our current culture is reminiscent of much of what Christ is describing in these verses.

This is the very point Driscoll made with his "war" reference, which he expanded on. "There's political wars, there's financial wars, there's real wars, there's terrorist wars, there's cultural wars, there's social wars, there's moral wars," he added. "I mean, I think people are battle-fatigued . . . you turn on your phone every day [and] you're like, 'Oh, gosh, what's the war today?'"[2]

And as these flammable cultural and political wars rage, understanding what's at the heart of the chaos and consternation seems key. Human nature opens us to individual and cultural sin, but the Bible also openly speaks of an "enemy" who seeks to destroy. When we look back at the biblical mentions of Satan covered in this book, we're confronted with some shocking descriptors that are worth briefly revisiting. The devil is referred to as an "enemy," "tempter," deceiver, and accuser who "prowls around like a roaring lion."

We have discussed Satan's impact as manifesting on an individual level, but Revelation 12:9 also speaks to the collective narrative, telling readers that the devil "leads the whole world astray." It's hard, then, not to wonder how this reality impacts our current cultural mayhem and the events unfolding under the spiritual surface—a reality comprehended most clearly through the lens of faith.

Reverend Samuel Rodriguez was among those consulted for this book who spoke to some of these broader themes, expressing his belief that "we are living in the last days"—and that we are watching this reality play out on a daily basis. "We are living in the dark days that the level of darkness is exponentially exacerbated. It's multiplied," he said. "That was laid out by the apostle Paul to Timothy. It's repeated throughout James, repeated throughout Revelation . . . and because we are living in the last days, darkness is increasing."

It's easy to dismiss events as unfolding in isolation, but what if something more uniform and pervasive is taking form, wreaking havoc, chaos, and intense pain in its path? What if there's a deeper conversation our material-obsessed culture is totally missing? "It may be that the culture wars and the political wars and the other wars are part of a much bigger war," Driscoll warned.

How Confusion Is Overtaking Our Culture

Since 2000, American culture has dramatically transformed, with a once more morally in-tune populace—one that was deeply impacted by the Judeo-Christian tradition—suddenly embracing relativistic perspectives on an array of important issues. From fact confusion to ethical uncertainty, America, like many other nations around the world, has continued to shift its moral center away from God and toward the self; it's a problematic change that has impacted the secular world on almost every discernible level.

Moving from a more collective conscience with a clearer and less unbridled sense of right and wrong to one in which morality is increasingly seen as fluid and influx, contemporary America is markedly different from the United States of not so long ago. As technology has increased, so has access to media and entertainment content—two arenas known for their progressive and secular bents.

My book *Fault Line: How a Seismic Shift in Culture Is Threatening Free Speech and Shaping the Next Generation* dives deep into the impact that Hollywood, media, and university culture has had on Americans, exploring how the triangular ideological dominance in these fields has collectively chipped away at the moral standards Americans once held dear.

Over time, information has transformed hearts and minds—and there's a social and spiritual cost to this litany of biased content. Much of what individuals have been consuming has slowly transformed our belief systems. As a result of these quick transitions, many Christians feel as though they've woken up in the middle of nowhere, searching for answers and solutions to these challenges. But as believers look for solutions, we must also understand the weight of these transformations.

"Oftentimes we look at the ballot box as being the solution to the problem. The ballot box is necessary, but it's not sufficient," Hank

Hanegraaff told me. "The things that change culture oftentimes have to do with the entertainment, educational, and environmental industries that create, manipulate, and disseminate ideological constructs . . . and when the culture is changed, what it does is it opens up avenues for the Prince of Darkness in many, many different ways."

"The only real solution to a disintegrating West is the power of the gospel of Jesus Christ," he added.

Regardless of whether one believes in Satan or sees the devil as a catalyst for various social problems, there are some undeniable facts about the current state of affairs. Americans today have an innate sense that something isn't quite right, with 49 percent of the country rating moral values in the US as "poor"—a record since Gallup started measuring in 2002.[3] Meanwhile, 37 percent rate moral values "only fair," with 14 percent saying they are "good" or "excellent."

But there's a real conundrum deep in Gallup's research: "While Americans . . . have shifted a great deal toward saying many issues are morally acceptable, the vast majority continue to believe moral values overall are worsening." There's clearly a disconnect; strangely, as the public liberalizes, it collectively feels as though morals are continuously denigrating.

This dynamic becomes even more evident when we start to explore perspective changes on specific moral issues, with Gallup asking Americans to give their views on whether something is "morally acceptable or morally wrong," regardless of whether or not respondents believe it should be legal.[4]

Some of the indicators show just how starkly our culture has changed—and in a relatively short time frame. While 53 percent of Americans felt sex between an unmarried woman and man was morally acceptable back in 2001, that proportion swelled to 69 percent in 2018. Likewise, the percentage of people saying that having a baby outside of marriage is morally acceptable increased from 45 percent in 2002 to 65 percent in 2018.

Divorce, too, has tragically seen a major uptick in moral support, with the proportion believing in its ethical merits increasing from 59 percent in 2001 to 76 percent in 2018.[5] Even polygamy—a stranger and less prevalent cultural issue (but one that is on the rise with the emergence of a three-person romantic relationship known as a "thruple")—saw moral support surge from 7 percent in 2003 to 19 percent in 2018.

It has been within the past eight years in particular that the pace of cultural change has been on steroids. Consider that 30 percent of Americans said that pornography was morally acceptable in 2011; seven years later, that proportion hit 43 percent.[6] Meanwhile, the majority of Americans have also decided they no longer want the government to promote traditional values, opting, instead, for the government to remain neutral.

While 57 percent of Americans wanted the government to promote traditional values back in 1993, 37 percent said they wanted to see the government remain neutral. Flash-forward to 2017 and 51 percent opted for "remain neutral" over the 45 percent who wanted to see the promotion of traditional values.[7] These numbers quantify the cultural ripples of immorality that people—and, in particular, Christians—have felt and discussed over the past few decades.

The prevalence and increase of secularism and anti-gospel perspectives through messaging and entertainment dovetails perfectly with these relativistic changes, but what's driving those changes? Is something deeper bubbling under the spiritual surface? If we take the Bible seriously and believe Ephesians 6—that we are up against "the spiritual forces of evil"—then there is certainly much to discuss.

Some of you might be reading this and scoffing over the notion that Satan has the power to sway culture. But if we consider that each individual heart can be impacted—and we look at the slant of the messages inundating us from Hollywood and media alone—it's logical to conclude that the collective whole could also be easily swayed, especially as alternative messages are snuffed out.

Ephesians 6:11–12 reminds believers to "put on the full armor of God" so that each person can "stand against the devil's schemes." In a culture that tells us we need no such armor and that anything goes, are we truly able to steadily stand? If we're told that "our struggle is not against flesh and blood, but against the rulers, against the authorities, against the powers of this dark world and against the spiritual forces of evil in the heavenly realms," are we taking that warning seriously if we apathetically sit idle?

Paul affirmed in 2 Corinthians 4:4 that "the god of this age has blinded the minds of unbelievers, so that they cannot see the light of the gospel that displays the glory of Christ, who is the image of God." If our culture is blind, perhaps theologians and pastors are right to conclude that there is a slippery cultural slope that has helped catapult our society into confusion.

Right now, nearly every arena of culture has been touched by spiritual disarray—and that includes the church. Christianity's once dominant place in society previously cultivated a scenario in which certain biblical values and perspectives were widely embraced or at least respected, even among atheists, agnostics, or the spiritually apathetic. But with the rapid secularization of culture has come an erosion of those values, as evidenced by the shocking statistics presented earlier in this chapter.

Unfortunately, these negative changes are not simply limited to the general culture, as many Christians, too, have become deeply confused when it comes to the gospel, with strange and unbiblical beliefs seeping into the Christian conscience. On a theological level, this confusion is deeply troubling, with many believers shockingly taking their cues from the world around them rather than from Scripture—a world that the Bible tells us has become "blinded."

Here's one startling statistic that should leave us nothing short of gasping for air: according to the Barna Group: "Only 17 percent of Christians who consider their faith important and attend church regularly actually have a biblical worldview."[8] Yes, you read that correctly. Fewer than one in five devout Christians see the world through a clear spiritual lens—one that aligns with the Bible they claim to hold dear.

The troubling Barna study found that 61 percent of practicing Christians agree with at least some ideals embraced by New Spirituality; nearly three in ten (28 percent) strongly agreed that every person is praying to the same spirit or god (no matter what name is used to appeal to that spiritual being).

And it doesn't end there. More than half—54 percent—found at least some agreement with postmodernist ideals, the belief that we can only know what's best for ourselves and that we're limited based on our own experience.

Finally, 36 percent of Christians embraced some thoughts espoused by Marxism, with 29 percent adhering to secularist ideologies.[9]

Brooke Hempell, senior vice-president of research at Barna, responded to the research by noting that it's "striking" how pervasive these ideals are among practicing Christians. "What stood out most to us was how stark the shift was between the Boomer and Gen-Xer generations. We expected Millennials to be most influenced by other worldviews, but the most dramatic increase in support for these ideals occurs with the generation before them," Hempell said. "It's no surprise, then, that the impact we see today in our social fabric is so pervasive, given that these ideas have been taking root for two generations."[10]

This data only scratches the surface when it comes to measuring the ways in which some facets of Christian culture are also coming apart at the seams. And while much of the focus has been on cultural changes and their impact on moral viewpoints, a related issue that has been given less attention is the impact it has had on politics and the level of dysfunction, immorality, and chaos that people are now willing to embrace—or, at the least, look past—in our political system.

In a world in which more people are saying, "The only truth you know is the truth you experience" and, "Anything goes so long as it doesn't impact me," the natural progression is a political realm in which the chosen candidates are suddenly unrestrained from the moral and ethical limitations that once governed the electoral process. This is all a rabbit hole that we can continue to travel down, but to return to Hanegraaff's point, the loss of truth in our culture could leave us with sweeping ramifications, particularly on the spiritual warfare front.

"Western civilization has been an incredible light to the world. . . . what if Jesus had never lived? We wouldn't have the medical institutions that we have today. We wouldn't have many of the societal benefits that we're experiencing in terms of liberation and equality, the liberation of people from slavery, the liberation of women, all of that resulted from the Christian ethic," he said. "When you start to lose that in a culture, and when you start to lose the language ethic of a culture where words don't mean what they once meant, when vocabulary starts to change, then you open up huge vistas for the evil one and his minions to operate within."

So, what's the solution to these transformations? Rodriguez said that Christians have the power to "turn on the light and shine brighter," even amid these challenging spiritual times. And he warned that the situation calls for some intact spiritual maturity. "I would argue there has never been more satanical darkening oppression like there is today," he said. "The level of spiritual warfare has increased exponentially because the enemy's camp is privy to the fact that this is the bottom of the ninth inning, two outs, no one's on base, and they trail by thirty runs. So, what does a wounded lion do?"

Rodriguez believes the devil aims to derail people through oppression and possession with the goal of taking as many people as possible to eternal condemnation, and he argued that it's time for the church to "wake up."

"The church has to have a wake-up call where we recognize that we're not just here . . . to preach the gospel and get people saved, which is great. That's the primary directive," he said, adding, though, that healing is also key. "[We must also] get people saved and delivered and healed, and the delivery part is delivered from spiritual oppression."

Regardless of where people stand, we're called to prayer as we confront these daily and diverse "wars," invocations not only for ourselves and our loved ones, but for the nation, culture, and world at large.

CONCLUSION
Extinguishing the Flames of Evil

It's nearly impossible to walk away from the biblical narrative unfazed by the captivating and convicting descriptions of the spiritual battles that rage on its illustrious pages. The pull described in Scripture that tugs at the hearts and minds of human beings and, in turn, transforms and oppresses nations and cultures, simply cannot be ignored.

Many will try to look away from these powerful currents, but we can see the evidence of their pervasiveness in our own natural intrigue—an innate interest that drives millions to flock to Hollywood horror flicks and to pay close attention when stories of unrestrained evil burst into the mainstream.

The Bible tells us these demonic evils are real, rather than mere fiction. Christians might disagree over the nature of evil, the ways in which it manifests, and the tools needed to combat it, but the biblical narrative makes it clear that dismissing the existence of Satan and associated wickedness simply isn't a choice for the biblically literate believer.

After researching the multitude of claims, scriptures, and opinions about the demonic realm that are presented in this book, I can't help but conclude that the biggest danger pertaining to spiritual warfare and its role in our lives is rooted in our own toxic apathy.

At the core of the matter, there's rabid material aloofness that tricks so many critics into denying the existence of good, evil, and everything in between.

This particular brand of indifference or even hostility toward truth—one that hyperfocuses on the temporal—tends to conceal diabolical forces, thus shielding their impact on our everyday lives and dismissing any and all claims of spiritual warfare as happenstance. Some in this camp might question why we don't see these demonic manifestations more vividly and routinely, which is an appropriate question to pose.

That said, there are some sufficient answers. If indeed it's true that there is an enemy who seeks to kill and destroy, why would that foe seek sunlight and attention? Wouldn't he prefer to continue lurking in the shadows, covertly wreaking havoc? Hiding, it seems, would be the more effective tactic, and many in the faith space agree. "It's a great tactic of the enemy to stay in the darkness," Grace Driscoll told *The Pure Flix Podcast*. "And if we bring him out into the light, it exposes a lot of his tactics."[1]

An obsession with the material incubates too many people from wanting to engage in the steps necessary to protect themselves and others. But the apathy or hostility of secularists isn't the only problem we face, as apathy within Christian circles also runs rampant. It's far too easy to blame the world for spiritual problems that the church has been tasked with (and failed at) helping solve.

Too many Christians, pastors, and churches have become complacent when it comes to discussing the full scope of the gospel, specifically the impact of spiritual warfare. God doesn't call us to have all of the answers, but to ignore a ministry that was clearly one of the most substantial parts of Jesus' earthly walk—all while we're pledging to try and live like Jesus did on that walk—seems strange and perplexing.

In addition to potentially causing us to miss some essential parts of the biblical narrative, ignoring the role and power of evil in our world also has other pitfalls, especially when it comes to processing God's love. Having proper "categories" for evil and good is essential to crafting human understanding, as Driscoll noted. "As a church, we need to be willing to have those categories of evil and holiness, because oftentimes God can get blamed for evil that happens if we don't have those categories," she said. "So, the danger in that is, 'Oh, God did this to me or God did that to me.'"

Driscoll continued, "No, we live in a fallen world with a very real enemy that loves to tempt and steal and kill and destroy, and so to have those categories is very helpful because then we also can have tools, the armor of God in Ephesians 6, to fight against the enemy's tactics. But if we don't have those categories, it kind of gets lumped into God, and it's not him."

In addition to obsessive secularism and biblical lethargy, intellectual apathy on the part of professed Christians can also be quite problematic. When we make definitive claims that everything in existence has demonic roots and that nothing stems from natural or physical causes, it can lead to skepticism and even worse, physical and spiritual malfeasance.

Finding the balance between mental and physical afflictions is necessary, as evidenced by nearly everyone presented in this text. From faith leaders to mental health providers, the consensus seems clear: a proper investigation of a person's afflictions is essential before concluding that something demonic is at the root.

We're clearly dealing with three forms of apathy that must be confronted: secularists' failure to embrace truth, Christians' dereliction of spiritual duty to confront truth, and believers' obsessive, hyperspiritual approach that alienates and expels intellect. In the end, it's about finding balance as we approach the Scriptures. If you've been reading *Playing with Fire* with intense skepticism and perhaps even the occasional eye roll, I'd challenge you to think more deeply.

Regardless of where you stand, recognizing the truths in Ephesians 6 is key. The Lord is powerful, and with the "full armor of God" we are able to take our "stand against the devil's schemes." Finally, truth calls us to Christ, and faith in Christ yields healing. The spiritual warfare discussion is about freedom, with Christ's death on the cross and his resurrection serving as the most transformational, curative measure in human history.

One of the common threads in all our discussions in *Playing with Fire* is that the power of Jesus' name is what yields true liberty—a reality that should come as no surprise when we study Christ's own words. Speaking to the Jews who believed in him, Jesus had a pertinent message: "If you hold to my teaching, you are really my disciples. Then you will know the truth, and the truth will set you free" (John 8:31–32. And he continued, "If the Son sets you free, you will be free indeed" (v. 36).

No matter where we stand on the spiritual warfare scale, one thing is universally true: we all need the Savior, as it is his power that helps us extinguish the flames of evil.

Believing in deliverance doesn't offer us salvation, but Scripture tells us that embracing Jesus and having a personal relationship with him can help heal our hearts and souls and can guarantee we spend eternity with Christ. And that's what truly matters.

Jesus broke down the importance of this dynamic:

> For God so loved the world that he gave his one and only Son, that whoever believes in him shall not perish but have eternal life. For God did not send his Son into the world to condemn the world, but to save the world through him. Whoever believes in him is not condemned, but whoever does not believe stands condemned

already because they have not believed in the name of God's one and only Son. This is the verdict: Light has come into the world, but people loved darkness instead of light because their deeds were evil. Everyone who does evil hates the light, and will not come into the light for fear that their deeds will be exposed. But whoever lives by the truth comes into the light, so that it may be seen plainly that what they have done has been done in the sight of God. (John 3:16–21)

Faith is a beautiful process—one that can protect us against spiritual chaos.

It is my hope and prayer that *Playing with Fire* will spark conversations about the differentiation between good and evil, and our role as Christians in helping people process through the realities of these dynamics.

I'll conclude with a verse that perfectly encapsulates the freedom that is available to us all: "Therefore, if anyone is in Christ, the new creation has come: The old has gone, the new is here!" (2 Corinthians 5:17).

And with that I say, "Amen."

ACKNOWLEDGMENTS

I would like to profoundly and formally thank the following individuals and organizations, as this book would have been an impossibility without their dedication, hard work, kindness, and support.

First and foremost, thank you, God, for continuing to amaze me by paving for me such a fascinating and rewarding career path—one that continues to surprise me. While I'm an imperfect person still learning and growing each day, I am increasingly blessed to learn the importance of truly relying on You to show me the path You want me on and, more importantly, what You want me to do for You.

Next, thank you to my wife, Andrea, and my two amazing daughters, Ava and Lilyana, for allowing me the time to work on this project. Andrea: you are the most patient, loving, and amazing wife. You put up with crazy schedules and endless conversation, and you're my biggest cheerleader. I thank God for you each and every day.

To my agent, Bill Jensen: your guidance has not only been informative, but it has been kind, missional, and above the call of duty. Thank you for the many phone calls, your decades of insight, and the support you so freely offer. I'm truly grateful for you.

And thank you to Emanate Books and Thomas Nelson for

allowing me to explore such a fundamentally important topic. *Playing with Fire* addresses subjects that might cause some to pause, yet your willingness to allow me to dive deep into this topic will hopefully open the floodgates of discussion and theological consideration.

I want to specifically thank my editor, Janene MacIvor, for keeping me on pace, on time, and on par with our end goal with this fulfilling project. Janene, you're a wonderful editor and I appreciate the time and care you gave to this project.

Thank you all for helping make this book a reality.

NOTES

Introduction: Pop Culture's Obsession with the Demonic

1. Richard Gallagher, "As a Psychiatrist, I Diagnose Mental Illness. Also, I Help Spot Demonic Possession," *Washington Post*, July 1, 2016, https://www .washingtonpost.com/posteverything/wp/2016/07/01/as-a-psychiatrist-i -diagnose-mental-illness-and-sometimes-demonic-possession/.

2. Gallagher, "As a Psychiatrist."

3. "In U.S., Decline of Christianity Continues at Rapid Pace," Pew Research Center, October 17, 2019, https://www.pewforum.org/2019/10/17 /in-u-s-decline-of-christianity-continues-at-rapid-pace/.

4. "Decline of Christianity," Pew Research Center.

5. Rebecca Rubin, "Diverse Audiences Are Driving the Horror Box Office Boom," *Variety*, October 25, 2018, https://variety.com/2018/film/box-office /horror-movies-study-1202994407/.

6. Rubin, "Diverse Audiences."

7. Rubin, "Diverse Audiences."

8. Jamie Ballard, "45% of Americans Believe That Ghosts and Demons Exist," YouGov, October 21, 2019, https://today.yougov.com/topics/lifestyle /articles-reports/2019/10/21/paranormal-beliefs-ghosts-demons-poll.

9. Ballard, "45% of Americans."

10. Ballard, "45% of Americans."

11. "CBS Poll: Could It Be Satan? Yes," *CBS News*, April 30, 1998, https://www .cbsnews.com/news/cbs-poll-could-it-be-satan-yes/.

12. "CBS Poll."

13. Katie Jagel, "Poll Results: Exorcism," YouGov, September 17, 2013, https://today.yougov.com/topics/philosophy/articles-reports/2013/09/17/poll-results-exorcism.

14. Jagel, "Poll Results."

15. Ballard, "45% of Americans."

16. Craig S. Keener, "Spiritual Possession as a Cross-Cultural Experience," *Bulletin for Biblical Research* 20.2 (2010), 215, http://www.pas.rochester.edu/~tim/study/Keener%20Possession%20.pdf.

17. Keener, "Spiritual Possession," 215.

18. Keener, "Spiritual Possession," 217.

19. Keener, "Spiritual Possession," 217–18.

20. Keener, "Spiritual Possession," 218.

21. Keener, "Spiritual Possession," 220–21.

22. Lauren Cahn, "12 Real Life Exorcisms That Actually Happened," *Reader's Digest*, accessed February 15, 2020, https://www.rd.com/culture/real-life-exorcisms/.

23. Marisa Kwiatkowski, "Exorcism: The Story Behind the Story," *Indy Star*, updated November 4, 2014, https://www.indystar.com/story/news/2014/10/31/exorcism-story-behind-story/18211747/.

Chapter One: *The Exorcist*

1. *The Exorcist*, directed by William Friedkin (Burbank, CA: Warner Bros., 1973).

2. Dr. Arnold T. Blumberg, "How 'The Exorcist' Redefined the Horror Genre," Fandom.com, October 25, 2016, https://www.fandom.com/articles/exorcist-redefined-horror-genre.

3. Edward B. Fiske, "'Exorcist' Adds Problems for Catholic Clergymen," *New York Times*, January 28, 1974, https://www.nytimes.com/1974/01/28/archives/-exorcist-adds-problems-for-catholic-clergymen.html.

4. Susan King, "William Peter Blatty Reflects on the 40th Anniversary of 'The Exorcist,'" *Los Angeles Times*, October 8, 2013, https://www.latimes.com/entertainment/movies/moviesnow/la-et-mn-william-peter-blatty-exorcist-20131008-story.html#axzz2jDSRIcjN.

5. John McGuire, "The St. Louis Exorcism of 1949: The Real-Life Inspiration for 'The Exorcist,'" *St. Louis Post-Dispatch*, October 28, 2019, https://www.stltoday.com/news/archives/the-st-louis-exorcism-of-the-real-life-inspiration-for/article_fbdecb6a-9d3c-5903-a12c-effd4f7a7713.html.

6. "SLU Legends and Lore: The 1949 St. Louis Exorcism," Saint Louis University News, October 30, 2019, https://www.slu.edu/news/2019/october/slu-legends-lore-exorcism.php.

7. "SLU Legends and Lore."

8. "SLU Legends and Lore."

9. "SLU Legends and Lore."

10. Bill Brinkley, "Priest Frees Mt. Rainier Boy Reported Held in Devil's Grip," *Washington Post*, August 20, 1949, https://www.washingtonpost.com/wp-srv/style/longterm/movies/features/dcmovies/exorcism1949.htm.

11. Brinkley, "Priest Frees Mt. Rainier Boy."

12. "SLU Legends and Lore."

13. Gregory J. Holman, "An Expert on the Real-Life Event That Inspired 'The Exorcist' Is Coming to Springfield," *Springfield News-Leader*, October 3, 2017, https://www.news-leader.com/story/entertainment/2017/10/03/expert-real-life-event-inspired-the-exorcist-coming-springfield/693507001/.

14. "SLU Legends and Lore."

15. "SLU Legends and Lore."

16. McGuire, "St. Louis Exorcism of 1949."

17. "Front Page, 1949: Boy 'Freed . . . of Possession by the Devil,'" *Washington Post*, accessed February 15, 2020, https://www.washingtonpost.com/archive/local/2000/10/21/front-page-1949-boy-freed-of-possession-by-the-devil/e3567d03-f076-400a-9fa4-af77f9791da2/.

18. Brinkley, "Priest Frees Mt. Rainier Boy."

19. Brinkley, "Priest Frees Mt. Rainier Boy."

20. Steve Head, "Interview with The Exorcist Writer/Producer William Peter Blatty," IGN, updated May 20, 2012, https://www.ign.com/articles/2000/09/20/interview-with-the-exorcist-writerproducer-william-peter-blatty.

21. Head, "Interview with the Exorcist Writer/Producer."

22. McGuire, "St. Louis Exorcism of 1949."

23. Head, "Interview with the Exorcist Writer/Producer."

24. McGuire, "St. Louis Exorcism of 1949."

Chapter Two: The Indiana Case

1. Marisa Kwiatkowski, "The Exorcisms of Latoya Ammons," *Indy Star*, January 25, 2014, https://www.indystar.com/story/news/2014/01/25/the-disposession-of-latoya-ammons/4892553/.

2. Kwiatkowski, "Exorcisms of Latoya Ammons."

3. Kwiatkowski, "Exorcisms of Latoya Ammons."

4. Kwiatkowski, "Exorcisms of Latoya Ammons."

5. Kwiatkowski, "Exorcisms of Latoya Ammons."

6. "Intake Officer's Report of Preliminary Inquiry and Investigation: Latoya Ammons," State of Indiana Police Department, April 20, 2012, https://www.documentcloud.org/documents/1004899-intake -officers-report.html.

7. "Intake Officer's Report."

8. "Intake Officer's Report."

9. Kwiatkowski, "Exorcisms of Latoya Ammons."

10. "Intake Officer's Report."

11. "Intake Officer's Report."

12. Kwiatkowski, "Exorcisms of Latoya Ammons."

13. Marisa Kwiatkowski, "Zak Bagans, Priest Disagree About 'Demon House,'" *Indy Star*, March 12, 2018, https://www.indystar.com/story /entertainment/2018/03/12/ghost-adventures-host-zak-bagans-demon -house-movie-set-indiana-home-warns-view-own-risk-trailer/407019002/.

14. Kwiatkowski, "Exorcisms of Latoya Ammons."

15. Kwiatkowski, "Exorcisms of Latoya Ammons."

16. Laura Collins, "Inside the 'Portal to Hell': Relative Gives Investigators Tour of Haunted Indiana Home Where 'Possessed' Children Were 'Chanting Satanically' and Saw 'Ugly, Black Monster," *Daily Mail*, updated January 31, 2014, https://www.dailymail.co.uk/news/article-2547224/EXCLUSIVE -A-portal-hell-Police-chief-priest-examined-possessed-children-haunted -Indiana-home-official-reports-saying-no-hoax.html.

17. Collins, "Inside the 'Portal to Hell.'"

18. Billy Hallowell, "Priest Who Performed Reported Exorcisms in Terrifying Indiana Case Doubles Down—and the Reporter Who Broke the Story Speaks Out," *The Blaze*, January 30, 2014, https://www.theblaze.com /news/2014/01/30/something-unworldly-indiana-exorcism-priest-doubles -down-on-demon-possession-story-as-bill-oreilly-presses-for-answers.

19. Kwiatkowski, "Exorcisms of Latoya Ammons."

20. "Exorcism," United States Conference of Catholic Bishops, accessed February 15, 2020, http://www.usccb.org/prayer-and-worship/sacraments -and-sacramentals/sacramentals-blessings/exorcism.cfm.

21. "Alleged Demon Home Sells for $35,000," *Courier Journal*, January 30, 2014,

https://www.courier-journal.com/story/news/local/indiana/2014/01/30
/alleged-demon-home-sells-for-35000/5058393/.

22. Kwiatkowski, "Exorcisms of Latoya Ammons."

23. Kwiatkowski, "Exorcisms of Latoya Ammons."

24. Sarah Bahr and Marisa Kwiatkowski, "Zak Bagans' 'Demon House' the Real Story: 10 Things to Know About the Gary, Indiana, Case," *Indy Star*, updated February 16, 2019, https://www.indystar.com/story/news/2018/12/28 /zak-bagans-demon-house-real-story-10-things-know-gary-indiana-latoya -ammons/2430585002/.

25. "Alleged Demon Home Sells."

Chapter Three: Cranmer's Claims

1. Billy Hallowell, "A Horrific Death-like Stench: Family Claims Demon Infested Their Home and Nearly Destroyed Their Lives," *The Blaze*, February 27, 2014, https://www.theblaze.com/news/2014/02/27/a-horrific-death-like-stench -family-claims-demon-infested-their-home-and-nearly-destroyed-their-lives.

2. Hallowell, "A Horrific Death-like Stench."

3. *Merriam-Webster*, s.v. "infest (v.)," accessed February 20, 2020, https://www .merriam-webster.com/dictionary/infest.

4. Sean D. Hamill, "Former Residents of Brentwood 'Demon' House Dispute Book's Claims," *Pittsburgh Post-Gazette*, October 25, 2014, https://www.post -gazette.com/local/south/2014/10/26/Former-residents-of-Brentwood -demon-house-dispute-book-s-claims/stories/201410210213.

5. Stephanie Hacke, "Evidence Gives Support to Tales of Local History in South Hills Area," *Trib Live*, March 6, 2013, https://archive.triblive.com /news/evidence-gives-support-to-tales-of-local-history-in-south-hills-area/.

6. Hacke, "Evidence Gives Support to Tales."

7. Hamill, "Former Residents of Brentwood."

8. Hamill, "Former Residents of Brentwood."

9. Hamill, "Former Residents of Brentwood."

Chapter Four: Satan's Nature and Impact

1. Timothy Mackie, "Book of Job: What's Going on Here?," Bible Project (blog), May 20, 2017, https://bibleproject.com/blog/book-job-whats-going/.

2. Mackie, "Book of Job."

3. "Book of Job," GotQuestions.org, accessed February 20, 2020, https://www .gotquestions.org/Book-of-Job.html.

NOTES

Chapter Five: What Demons Are

1. David Jeremiah, "Angels and Demons Q&A," David Jeremiah (blog), accessed February 20, 2020, https://davidjeremiah.blog/angels -and-demons-qa/.

2. Billy Hallowell, "Bible Scholar Explains Why Everything You've Been Taught About Demons Might Be Completely Wrong," *The Blaze*, October 30, 2015, https://www.theblaze.com/news/2015/10/30/bible-scholar -explains-why-everything-many-christians-have-been-taught-about -demons-is-completely-wrong.

3. Hallowell, "Bible Scholar Explains."

4. Hallowell, "Bible Scholar Explains."

5. Matt Slick, "Where in the Bible Does It Say That One-Third of the Angels Fell?," Christian Apologetics and Research Ministry, August 9, 2009, https://carm.org/where-bible-does-it-say-one-third-angels-fell.

6. Slick, "Where in the Bible?"

7. "Do Angels Have Free Will?," GotQuestions.org, accessed February 20, 2020, https://www.gotquestions.org/angels-free-will.html.

8. "Do Angels Have Free Will?"

9. "Do Angels Have Free Will?"

10. Jeremiah, "Angels and Demons."

11. *Encyclopedia Britannica Online*, s.v. "First Book of Enoch," updated February 12, 2020, https://www.britannica.com/topic/First-Book-of-Enoch.

12. "Who Was Enoch in the Bible?," GotQuestions.org, accessed February 20, 2020, https://www.gotquestions.org/Enoch-in-the-Bible.html.

13. Michael L. Brown, "Why Isn't the Book of Enoch in the Bible?," Ask Dr. Brown (blog), June 20, 2016, https://askdrbrown.org/library/why -isn%E2%80%99t-book-enoch-bible.

14. Brown, "Why Isn't the Book of Enoch in the Bible?"

15. Brown, "Why Isn't the Book of Enoch in the Bible?"

16. Brown, "Why Isn't the Book of Enoch in the Bible?"

17. Ellen White, "Who Are the Nephilim?," Biblical Archaeology Society, September 30, 2019, https://www.biblicalarchaeology.org/daily /biblical-topics/hebrew-bible/who-are-the-nephilim/.

18. White, "Who Are the Nephilim?"

19. Michael S. Heiser, "Where Do Demons Come From?," Logos Talk (blog), October 28, 2015, https://blog.logos.com/2015/10/where-do-demons -come-from/.

20. White, "Who Are the Nephilim?"

21. Megan Sauter, "Rock Giants in Noah," Biblical Archaeology Society, October 1, 2019, https://www.biblicalarchaeology.org/daily/biblical-topics /hebrew-bible/rock-giants-in-noah/.

22. Sauter, "Rock Giants in Noah."

23. Sauter, "Rock Giants in Noah."

24. "Book of Enoch," Wesley Center Online, accessed February 21, 2020, http://wesley.nnu.edu/index.php?id=2126.

25. "Book of Enoch."

26. Hallowell, "Bible Scholar Explains."

27. Hallowell, "Bible Scholar Explains."

28. Heiser, "Where Do Demons Come From?"

29. Heiser, "Where Do Demons Come From?"

30. "Book of Enoch."

Chapter Six: Jesus and Demonic Possession

1. "Why Are There Two Demon-Possessed Men in the Gerasene Tomb in Matthew, But Only One in Mark and Luke?," GotQuestions.org, accessed February 21, 2020, https://www.gotquestions.org/one-two-demoniacs .html.

2. "Why Are There Two Demon-Possessed Men?"

3. "Who Was Mary Magdalene?," GotQuestions.org, accessed February 21, 2020, https://www.gotquestions.org/Mary-Magdalene.html.

Chapter Seven: Pathways to Spiritual Quicksand

1. "Why Did God Send an Evil Spirit to Torment King Saul?," GotQuestions. org, accessed February 21, 2020, https://www.gotquestions.org/evil-spirit -Saul.html.

2. "Why Did God Send an Evil Spirit?"

3. Richard McDonald, "'God Made Me Do It!' Why Did God Tempt Saul with an Evil Spirit?," The Gospel Coalition, October 3, 2019, https://www .thegospelcoalition.org/article/god-made-god-tempt-saul-evil-spirit/.

4. Matt Slick, "What Is Demonic Oppression?," Christian Apologetics and Research Ministry, October 17, 2014, https://carm.org/questions /about-demons/what-demonic-oppression.

5. Slick, "What Is Demonic Oppression?"

6. Slick, "What Is Demonic Oppression?"

7. *Merriam-Webster*, s.v. "prophet (*n.*)," accessed February 21, 2020, https://www.merriam-webster.com/dictionary/prophet.

8. Matt Slick, "Can Drug Use Cause Demonic Possession?," Christian Apologetics and Research Ministry, accessed February 21, 2020, https://carm.org/can-drug-use-cause-demonic-possession.

9. Slick, "Can Drug Use Cause Demonic Possession?"

Chapter Eight: The Ouija Board

1. "Ouija Board Game Customer Review: Stephanie Bertrine," Amazon, November 25, 2018, https://www.amazon.com/gp/customer -reviews/R3VO7HE2EE3GRU/ref=cm_cr_arp_d_rvw _ttl?ie=UTF8&ASIN=B01BDK1O64.

2. "Ouija Board Game Customer Review: Salman Rahman," Amazon, January 31, 2018, https://www.amazon.com/gp/customer-reviews /RM64N6SSXVTOY/ref=cm_cr_getr_d_rvw_ttl?ie=UTF8&ASIN =B01BDK1O64.

3. "Ouija Board Game Customer Review: Taylor L.," Amazon, January 14, 2018, https://www.amazon.com/gp/customer-reviews/R9ACXDXZ9FYW9 /ref=cm_cr_getr_d_rvw_ttl?ie=UTF8&ASIN=B01BDK1O64.

4. "Ouija Game Description," Hasbro Shop, accessed February 21, 2020, https://shop.hasbro.com/en-us/product/ouija-game:86117134-5056-9047-F5E1 -46EB2553A56A.

5. "Ouija, or the Wonderful Talking Board," advertisement, *Pittsburgh Dispatch*, February 1, 1891, page 12, accessed by Penn State University Libraries, https://chroniclingamerica.loc.gov/lccn/sn84024546/1891-02-01/ed-1 /seq-12/#date1=1836&sort=date&date2=1922&words=Board+Ouija&searc hType=basic&sequence=0&index=0&state=&rows=20&proxtext=ouija +board&y=0&x=0&dateFilterType=yearRange&page=1.

6. Neil Tweedie, "Sales of Ouija Boards Up 300% and Threatening to Become a Christmas 'Must Buy' Despite Warning from Churchmen," *Daily Mail*, November 30, 2014, https://www.dailymail.co.uk/news/article-2855439 /Sales-Ouija-boards-300-threatening-Christmas-buy-despite-Church -England-warning.html.

7. Tweedie, "Sales of Ouija Boards."

8. Tweedie, "Sales of Ouija Boards."

9. Linda Rodriguez McRobbie, "The Strange and Mysterious History of the Ouija Board," *Smithsonian*, October 27, 2013, https://www.smithsonianmag

.com/history/the-strange-and-mysterious-history-of-the-ouija-board
-5860627/?no-ist.

10. McRobbie, "Strange and Mysterious History."

11. McRobbie, "Strange and Mysterious History."

12. McRobbie, "Strange and Mysterious History."

13. "E. J. Bond: Toy or Game," United States Patent and Trademark Office, February 10, 1891,https://pdfpiw.uspto.gov/.piw?PageNum =0&docid=00446054&IDKey=538D3AFB15E8%0D%0A&HomeUrl =http%3A%2F%2Fpatft.uspto.gov%2Fnetahtml%2FPTO%2Fpatimg.htm.

14. "The Ouija: The Wonder of the Nineteenth Century," advertisement, *The Sunday Herald*, December 21, 1890, page 2, accessed by the Library of Congress, https://chroniclingamerica.loc.gov/lccn/sn82016373/1890-12-21 /ed-1/seq-2/?date1=1890&index=0&date2=1891&searchType=advanced&pr oxdistance=5&rows=20&ortext=&proxtext=&phrasetext=&andtext=ouija +board&dateFilterType=yearRange#words=board%2BOUIJA.

15. Olivia B. Waxman, "*Ouija: Origin of Evil* and the True History of the Ouija Board," *Time*, October 21, 2016, https://time.com/4529861/ouija -board-history-origin-of-evil/.

16. "The Planchette Craze Has Broken Out Again," *The Morning Call*, November 14, 1893, page 8, accessed by the University of California, https://chroniclingamerica.loc.gov/lccn/sn94052989/1893 -11-14/ed-1/seq-8/?date1=1836&index=1&date2=1922&searc hType=advanced&proxdistance=5&rows=20&ortext=&pro xtext=&phrasetext=&andtext=seance+planchette&dateFi lterType=yearRange#words=Planchette%2Bplanchette%2Bseances.

17. McRobbie, "Strange and Mysterious History."

18. "Ouija Board Inventor Dies in Fall off Roof; Fuld Loses His Balance While Placing New Flag Pole on His Baltimore Toy Factory," *New York Times*, February 27, 1927, https://www.nytimes.com/1927/02/27/archives/ouija -board-inventor-dies-in-fall-off-roof-fuld-loses-his-balance.html.

19. "Ouija Board Inventor Dies."

20. McRobbie, "Strange and Mysterious History."

21. Baynard Woods, "The Ouija Board's Mysterious Origins: War, Spirits, and a Strange Death," *The Guardian*, October 30, 2016, https://www.theguardian .com/lifeandstyle/2016/oct/30/ouija-board-mystery-history.

22. McRobbie, "Strange and Mysterious History."

23. Waxman, "*Ouija: Origin of Evil.*"

24. Joseph P. Laycock, "How the Ouija Board Got Its Sinister Reputation," *Associated Press*, October 18, 2016, https://apnews.com /ddbdb09b485542ecac14758619674af2.

25. Laycock, "How the Ouija Board Got Its Sinister Reputation."

26. David J. Krajicek, "The Ouija Board Murder: Tricking Tribal Healer Nancy Bowen to Kill," *New York Daily News*, March 21, 2010, https://www .nydailynews.com/news/crime/ouija-board-murder-tricking-tribal -healer-nancy-bowen-kill-article-1.175705.

27. Krajicek, "The Ouija Board Murder."

28. Krajicek, "The Ouija Board Murder."

29. Scott G. Eberle, "The Ouija Board Explained," *Psychology Today*, May 16, 2012, https://www.psychologytoday.com/us/blog/play-in-mind/201205 /the-ouija-board-explained.

30. Eberle, "The Ouija Board Explained."

31. Eberle, "The Ouija Board Explained."

32. Aja Romano, "How Ouija Boards Work. (Hint: It's Not Ghosts.)," *Vox*, updated September 6, 2018, https://www.vox.com/2016/10/29/13301590 /how-ouija-boards-work-debunked-ideomotor-effect.

33. Romano, "How Ouija Boards Work."

34. Julia Layton, "How Ouija Boards Work," *How Stuff Works*, accessed February 21, 2020, https://science.howstuffworks.com/science-vs-myth/unexplained -phenomena/ouija-boards4.htm.

35. William Fuld, as quoted in Mitch Horowitz, *Occult America: The Secret History of How Mysticism Shaped Our Nation* (New York: Bantam Books, 2009), 72.

Chapter Nine: Do Ghosts Really Exist?

1. *Merriam-Webster*, s.v. "ghost (n.)," accessed February 22, 2020, https://www .merriam-webster.com/dictionary/ghost.

2. Jamie Ballard, "45% of People Believe That Ghosts and Demons Exist," *YouGov*, October 21, 2019, https://today.yougov.com/topics/lifestyle /articles-reports/2019/10/21/paranormal-beliefs-ghosts-demons-poll.

3. Russell Heimlich, "See Dead People," Pew Research Center, December 29, 2009, https://www.pewresearch.org/fact-tank/2009/12/29/see-dead-people/.

4. Michael Lipka, "18% of Americans Say They've Seen a Ghost," Pew Research Center, October 30, 2015, https://www.pewresearch.org/fact -tank/2015/10/30/18-of-americans-say-theyve-seen-a-ghost/.

5. Emily McFarlan Miller, "What Does the Bible Say About Ghosts?," *Relevant*, October 31, 2019, https://relevantmagazine.com/god/what-does-bible -say-about-ghosts-i/.

6. Miller, "What Does the Bible Say?"

7. "What Happens After Death?," GotQuestions.org, accessed February 22, 2020, https://www.gotquestions.org/what-happens-death.html.

8. Lipka, "18% of Americans."

9. Ron Rhodes, as quoted in Rick Barry, "Do You Believe in Ghosts?," *Answers*, October 28, 2014, https://answersingenesis.org/angels-and -demons/do-you-believe-in-ghosts/.

10. Miller, "What Does the Bible Say?"

11. "Does My Soul Sleep After Death?: Interview with John Piper," DesiringGod.org, April 7, 2016, https://www.desiringgod.org/interviews /does-my-soul-sleep-after-death.

12. "Does My Soul Sleep After Death?"

13. "Does My Soul Sleep After Death?"

14. John Piper, "Split Rocks, Open Tombs, Raised Bodies: What Happened in the Graveyards Outside Jerusalem?," DesiringGod.org, April 15, 2017, https://www.desiringgod.org/articles/split-rocks-open-tombs-raised-bodies.

15. John Greco, "The Other Resurrection: Matthew's Troubling Account of the Dead Who Were Raised on Good Friday," *In Touch Ministries*, February 20, 2016, https://www.intouch.org/read/magazine/margin-notes/the-other -resurrection.

16. "Did the Witch of Endor Really Summon Samuel from the Dead (1 Samuel 28: 7–20)?," GotQuestions.org, accessed February 22, 2020, https://www .gotquestions.org/witch-of-endor.html.

17. Rick Barry, "Do You Believe in Ghosts?," *Answers*, October 28, 2014, https://answersingenesis.org/angels-and-demons/do-you-believe-in-ghosts/.

Chapter Ten: Exorcism and Deliverance

1. Peter Finney Jr., "Priest Says Exorcism Is Ministry of Healing That Helps Suffering People," *Crux Catholic Media*, October 25, 2017, https://cruxnow .com/church-in-the-usa/2017/10/priest-says-exorcism-ministry-healing -helps-suffering-people/.

2. Rebecca Traister, "The Exorcist," *Salon*, January 18, 2005, https://www .salon.com/2005/01/18/peck_5/.

3. Traister, "The Exorcist."

4. "Exorcism," United States Conference of Catholic Bishops, accessed February 15, 2020, http://www.usccb.org/prayer-and-worship/sacraments -and-sacramentals/sacramentals-blessings/exorcism.cfm.

5. "Exorcism," USCCB.

6. Catholic News Service, "US Bishops Publish English-Language Translation of Exorcism Ritual," *Catholic Herald*, October 25, 2017, https ://catholicherald.co.uk/news/2017/10/25/us-bishops-publish-english -language-translation-of-exorcism-ritual/.

7. John Tagliabue, "The Pope's Visit: The Doctrine; Vatican's Revised Exorcism Rite Affirms Existence of Devil," *New York Times*, January 27, 1999, https://www.nytimes.com/1999/01/27/us/pope-s-visit-doctrine -vatican-s-revised-exorcism-rite-affirms-existence-of-devil.html.

8. Catholic News Service, "US Bishops."

9. Tagliabue, "The Pope's Visit."

10. Tagliabue, "The Pope's Visit."

11. Catholic News Service, "FAQs: What Is an Exorcism?," *Catholic Herald*, October 25, 2017, https://catholicherald.co.uk/commentandblogs /2017/10/25/faqs-what-is-an-exorcism/.

12. "Exorcism," USCCB.

13. "Exorcism," USCCB.

14. Conor Gaffey, "What is Exorcism? U.S. Catholic Bishops Have Just Translated Prayers to Cast Out Demons into English for the First Time," *Newsweek*, February 18, 2020, https://www.newsweek.com/what-exorcism -catholic-church-pope-francis-692410.

15. Nick Squires, "Exorcists from Across Christianity Gather to Trade Tips on Fighting Satan," *The Telegraph*, May 6, 2019, https://www.telegraph.co.uk /news/2019/05/06/exorcists-different-denominations-gather-firstz-time -trade-tips/.

16. "Exorcism," USCCB.

17. "Can a Christian Today Perform an Exorcism?," GotQuestions.org, accessed February 20, 2020, https://www.gotquestions.org/Christian-exorcism.html.

18. "Can a Christian Today Perform an Exorcism?"

19. "Can a Christian Today Perform an Exorcism?"

20. "Can a Christian Today Perform an Exorcism?"

21. Pat Robertson, "What is Exorcism? How Can a Demon Be Cast Out?" *Christian Broadcasting Network*, accessed February 20, 2020, https://www1 .cbn.com/questions/what-is-exorcism-demon-cast-out.

22. Robertson, "What is Exorcism?"

23. Robertson, "What is Exorcism?"

24. Traister, "The Exorcist."

25. Traister, "The Exorcist."

26. Barbie Latza Nadeau, "Vatican Assembles Avengers of Religion to Beat the Devil," *Daily Beast*, May 8, 2019, https://www.thedailybeast.com/vatican -exorcist-convention-tries-innovative-ways-to-beat-the-devil.

27. Nadeau, "Vatican Assembles Avengers."

28. Jack Wellman, "Are Deliverance Ministries Biblical?," *Christian Crier* (blog), August 18, 2017, https://www.patheos.com/blogs/christiancrier/2017/08/18 /are-deliverance-ministries-biblical/.

29. Wellman, "Are Deliverance Ministries Biblical?"

30. Wellman, "Are Deliverance Ministries Biblical?"

31. Wellman, "Are Deliverance Ministries Biblical?"

Chapter Eleven: Possession of Christians?

1. Paige Cushman, "'I Could See the Demons': An Exorcism in Arkansas," KATV News, October 29, 2019, https://katv.com/news/local/i-could -see-the-demons-an-exorcism-in-arkansas.

2. Jack Wellman, "Are Deliverance Ministries Biblical?," *Christian Crier* (blog), August 18, 2017, https://www.patheos.com/blogs/christiancrier/2017/08/18 /are-deliverance-ministries-biblical/.

3. Wellman, "Are Deliverance Ministries Biblical?"

4. Ray Pritchard, "What Happened to Judas?," Crosswalk.com, March 23, 2007, https://www.crosswalk.com/church/pastors-or-leadership/what-happened -to-judas-11532302.html.

5. Matt Slick, "Was Judas Saved or Did He Lose His Salvation?," Christian Apologetics and Research Ministry, October 17, 2014, https://carm.org /was-judas-saved-or-did-he-lose-his-salvation.

6. Pritchard, "What Happened to Judas?"

Chapter Thirteen: Possession Versus Illness

1. John Blake, "When Exorcists Need Help, They Call Him," CNN Health, August 4, 2017, https://www.cnn.com/2017/08/04/health/exorcism-doctor /index.html.

2. Blake, "When Exorcists Need Help."

3. Richard Gallagher, "As a Psychiatrist, I Diagnose Mental Illness. Also, I Help

NOTES

Spot Demonic Possession." *The Washington Post*, July 1, 2016, https://www
.washingtonpost.com/posteverything/wp/2016/07/01/as-a-psychiatrist
-i-diagnose-mental-illness-and-sometimes-demonic-possession/?utm
_source=reddit.com.

4. Gallagher, "As a Psychiatrist."
5. Gallagher, "As a Psychiatrist."
6. Blake, "When Exorcists Need Help."
7. Gallagher, "As a Psychiatrist."
8. Gallagher, "As a Psychiatrist."
9. Gallagher, "As a Psychiatrist."
10. Gallagher, "As a Psychiatrist."
11. Kay Bartlett, "'Encountered Satan' During Exorcisms: Psychiatrist Sees Evil as Form of Mental Illness," *Los Angeles Times*, December 15, 1985, https://www .latimes.com/archives/la-xpm-1985-12-15-mn-499-story.html.
12. Description found on Amazon for M. Scott Peck, *Glimpses of the Devil: A Psychiatrist's Personal Accounts of Possession* (New York: Simon and Schuster, 2005), https://www.amazon.com/Glimpses-Devil-Psychiatrists-Personal -Possession/dp/1439167265/ref=pd_cp_14_3/146-8870870-8172968?_encoding =UTF8&pd_rd_i=1439167265&pd_rd_r=2f457d07-be26-4287-98bd-93f2929 cb4fa&pd_rd_w=MAks6&pd_rd_wg=L9usD&pf_rd_p=0e5324e1-c848 -4872-bbd5-5be6baedf80e&pf_rd_r=PH3YR2JYW06PY6PB5SXY&psc=1 &refRID=PH3YR2JYW06PY6PB5SXY.
13. Description found on Amazon for M. Scott Peck, *Glimpses of the Devil*.
14. Rebecca Traister, "The Exorcist," *Salon*, January 18, 2005, https://www .salon.com/2005/01/18/peck_5/.
15. Bartlett, "'Encountered Satan' During Exorcisms."
16. Traister, "The Exorcist."
17. Bartlett, "'Encountered Satan' During Exorcisms."
18. Traister, "The Exorcist."
19. Traister, "The Exorcist."
20. Traister, "The Exorcist."
21. Blake, "When Exorcists Need Help."
22. Blake, "When Exorcists Need Help."
23. Mary D. Moller, "Incorporating Religion into Psychiatry: Evidence-Based Practice, Not a Bioethical Dilemma," *Narrative Inquiry into Bioethics* 4.3, (2014), 206–208, https://muse.jhu.edu/article/562724.
24. Moller, "Incorporating Religion into Psychiatry."

25. Moller, "Incorporating Religion into Psychiatry."

26. Moller, "Incorporating Religion into Psychiatry."

27. Moller, "Incorporating Religion into Psychiatry."

28. Moller, "Incorporating Religion into Psychiatry."

29. Marisa Iati and Kim Bellware, "A Man Drowned His 6-Year-Old Son While Trying to Cast Out a 'Demon,' Police Say," *The Washington Post*, October 4, 2019, https://www.washingtonpost.com/nation/2019/10/02/man-drowned -his-year-old-son-while-trying-cast-out-demon-police-say/.

30. Vicky Baker, "The 'Exorcism' That Turned into Murder," *BBC News*, February 28, 2018, https://www.bbc.co.uk/news/resources /idt-sh/nicaragua_exorcism_vilma_trujillo_murder.

31. Baker, "The 'Exorcism.'"

32. "Exorcism," United States Conference of Catholic Bishops, accessed February 15, 2020, http://www.usccb.org/prayer-and-worship/sacraments -and-sacramentals/sacramentals-blessings/exorcism.cfm.

33. "Article 1: Sacramentals," part 2, section 2, *Catechism of the Catholic Church*, accessed February 20, 2020, https://www.vatican.va/archive/ccc_css /archive/catechism/p2s2c4a1.htm.

34. "Article 1: Sacramentals."

35. Billy Hallowell, "Mark and Grace Driscoll Prepare You for 'Spiritual Battle,'" *The Pure Flix Podcast*, November 15, 2019, https://anchor.fm/pureflixpodcast /episodes/Mark-and-Grace-Driscoll-Prepare-You-for-Spiritual-Battle--and -the-Author-of-the-God-Gave-Us-Series-Drops-By-e911rh.

36. Joseph T. English, "Letter to the Editor: Demons and Posessions," *New Oxford Review*, June 2008, https://www.newoxfordreview.org/documents /letter-to-the-editor-june-2008/.

37. Hallowell, "Mark and Grace Driscoll."

Chapter Fourteen: Spiritual Impact on Our Culture

1. Billy Hallowell, "Mark and Grace Driscoll Prepare You for 'Spiritual Battle,'" *The Pure Flix Podcast*, November 15, 2019, https://anchor.fm/pureflixpodcast /episodes/Mark-and-Grace-Driscoll-Prepare-You-for-Spiritual-Battle--and -the-Author-of-the-God-Gave-Us-Series-Drops-By-e911rh.

2. Hallowell, "Mark and Grace Driscoll."

3. Justin McCarthy, "About Half of Americans Say U.S. Moral Values Are 'Poor,'" Gallup, June 1, 2018, https://news.gallup.com/poll/235211/half -americans-say-moral-values-poor.aspx.

NOTES

4. "Moral Issues," Gallup, accessed February 21, 2020, https://news.gallup
   .com/poll/1681/moral-issues.aspx.
5. "Moral Issues," Gallup.
6. Megan Brenan, "Slim Majority Against Government Pushing Traditional
   Values," Gallup, October 6, 2017, https://news.gallup.com/poll/220235/slim
   -majority-against-government-pushing-traditional-values.aspx.
7. Brenan, "Slim Majority."
8. "Competing Worldviews Influence Today's Christians," Barna Research,
   Culture and Media, May 9, 2017, https://www.barna.com/research
   /competing-worldviews-influence-todays-christians/.
9. "Competing Worldviews," Barna Research.
10. "Competing Worldviews," Barna Research.

Conclusion: Extinguishing the Flames of Evil

1. Billy Hallowell, "Mark and Grace Driscoll Prepare You for 'Spiritual Battle,'"
   The Pure Flix Podcast, November 15, 2019, https://anchor.fm/pureflixpodcast
   /episodes/Mark-and-Grace-Driscoll-Prepare-You-for-Spiritual-Battle--and
   -the-Author-of-the-God-Gave-Us-Series-Drops-By-e911rh.

ABOUT THE AUTHOR

Billy Hallowell has been working in journalism and media for more than two decades. His writings, interviews, and social commentary have appeared in the *Washington Post, Deseret News, TheBlaze, Human Events*, the *Christian Post, Mediaite*, and FoxNews.com, among other outlets. He is currently the director of communications and content at Pure Flix. Hallowell has served as the faith and culture editor of *TheBlaze*, senior editor of *Faithwire*, and has written four books. Hallowell has a BA in journalism and broadcasting from the College of Mount Saint Vincent in Riverdale, New York, and an MS in social research from Hunter College in Manhattan, New York. Billy and his family live just outside of New York City.